Karl Budde

Religion of Israel to the Exile

Karl Budde

Religion of Israel to the Exile

ISBN/EAN: 9783743311312

Manufactured in Europe, USA, Canada, Australia, Japa

Cover: Foto ©Lupo / pixelio.de

Manufactured and distributed by brebook publishing software (www.brebook.com)

Karl Budde

Religion of Israel to the Exile

THE AMERICAN LECTURES ON THE HISTORY OF RELIGIONS.

I. **Buddhism.**—The History and Literature of Buddhism. By T. W. RHYS-DAVIDS, LL.D., Ph.D.

II. **Primitive Religions.**—The Religions of Primitive Peoples. By D. G. BRINTON, A.M., M.D., LL.D., Sc.D., Professor of Archæology and Linguistics in the University of Pennsylvania.

III. **Israel.**—Jewish Religious Life After the Exile. By the Rev. T. K. CHEYNE, M.A., D.D., Oriel Professor of the Interpretation of the Holy Scriptures in the University of Oxford, and formerly Fellow of Balliol College ; Canon of Rochester.

IV. **Israel.**—The Religion of Israel to the Exile. By Professor KARL BUDDE, of Strasburg, Germany.

G. P. PUTNAM'S SONS
NEW YORK AND LONDON

*AMERICAN LECTURES ON THE
HISTORY OF RELIGIONS*

FOURTH SERIES—1898-1899

RELIGION OF ISRAEL TO THE EXILE

BY

KARL BUDDE, D.D.

Professor of Theology in Strassburg

G. P. PUTNAM'S SONS
NEW YORK AND LONDON
The Knickerbocker Press
1899

COPYRIGHT, 1899
BY
G. P. PUTNAM'S SONS

Entered at Stationers' Hall, London

The Knickerbocker Press, New York

ANNOUNCEMENT

THE American Lectures on the History of Religions are delivered under the auspices of the American Committee for Lectures on the History of Religions. This Committee was organised in 1892 for the purpose of instituting " popular courses in the History of Religions, somewhat after the style of the Hibbert lectures in England, to be delivered annually by the best scholars of Europe and this country, in various cities, such as Baltimore, Boston, Brooklyn, Chicago, New York, Philadelphia, and others."

The terms of association under which the Committee exists are as follows:

1.—The object of this Association shall be to provide courses of lectures on the history of religions, to be delivered in various cities.
2.—The Association shall be composed of delegates from Institutions agreeing to co-operate, or from Local Boards organised where such co-operation is not possible.
3.—These delegates—one from each Institution or Local Board—shall constitute themselves a

Council under the name of the " American Committee for Lectures on the History of Religions."

4.—The Council shall elect out of its number a President, a Secretary, and a Treasurer.

5.—All matters of local detail shall be left to the Institutions or Local Boards, under whose auspices the lectures are to be delivered.

6.—A course of lectures on some religion, or phase of religion, from an historical point of view, or on a subject germane to the study of religions, shall be delivered annually, or at such intervals as may be found practicable, in the different cities represented by this Association.

7.—The Council (a) shall be charged with the selection of the lecturers, (b) shall have charge of the funds, (c) shall assign the time for the lectures in each city, and perform such other functions as may be necessary.

8.—Polemical subjects, as well as polemics in the treatment of subjects, shall be positively excluded.

9.—The lecturer shall be chosen by the Council at least ten months before the date fixed for the course of lectures.

10.—The lectures shall be delivered in the various

cities between the months of October and June.

11.—The copyright of the lectures shall be the property of the Association.

12.—One half of the lecturer's compensation shall be paid at the completion of the entire course, and the second half upon the publication of the lectures.

13.—The compensation to the lecturer shall be fixed in each case by the Council.

14.—The lecturer is not to deliver elsewhere any of the lectures for which he is engaged by the Committee, except with the sanction of the Committee.

The Committee as now constituted is as follows:

C. H. Toy (Harvard University), Chairman.
Morris Jastrow, Jr. (University of Pa.), Secretary.
John P. Peters (New York), Treasurer.
Francis Brown (Union Theological Seminary).
Richard J. H. Gottheil (Columbia University).
Paul Haupt (Johns Hopkins University).
Franklin W. Hooper (Brooklyn Institute).
George F. Moore (Andover Theological Seminary).
F. K. Sanders (Yale University).
J. G. Schurman (Cornell University).
W. R. Harper (University of Chicago).

Announcement

The first course of American Lectures on the History of Religions was delivered in the winter of 1894-1895, by Prof. T. W. Rhys-Davids, Ph.D., LL.D., of London, England. His subject was the History and Literature of Buddhism. The second course was delivered in 1896-1897, by Prof. Daniel G. Brinton, A.M., M.D., LL.D., Sc.D., of Philadelphia, on the Religions of Primitive Peoples. The third course of lectures was delivered in 1897-1898, on Jewish Religious Life after the Exile, by the Rev. T. K. Cheyne, M.A., D.D., Oriel Professor of the Interpretation of Holy Scriptures at Oxford, and Canon of Rochester. These lectures were published in book form by Messrs. G. P. Putnam's Sons, publishers to the Committee, under the above titles, in 1896, 1897, and 1898, respectively.

The fourth course of lectures was delivered in 1898-1899, on the Religion of Israel to the Exile, by Prof. Karl Budde, D.D., of Strassburg, and is contained in the present volume.

Professor Karl Ferdinand Reinhardt Budde, Professor of Theology in Strassburg, is one of the best known Old Testament scholars of the present day. His principal writings are: *Beiträge zur Kritik des Buches Hiob ; Die Biblische Urgeschichte ; Die Bücher Richter und Samuel;* and Commentaries on *Job, Judges, Canticles, and Lamentations,* the first in

Announcement

Nowack's *Handkommentar* series, and the others in Marti's *Kurzer Handkommentar* series. He is also the editor and translator of the books of *Samuel* in Professor Haupt's polychrome edition of the *Sacred Books of the Old Testament*. In addition he translated into German Kuenen's *Hibbert Lectures on National Religions and Universal Religions*, and translated and edited the same scholar's *Gesammelte Abhandlungen*. He is also the author of a number of important papers in German and American publications, among which may be mentioned especially his *Folk-song of Israel*, *Song of the Well*, *Song of Solomon*, and *Nomadic Ideal in the Old Testament*, published in *The New World* (1893–1895), and an article on *Habakkuk* in *The Expositor* (1895).

The lecturer for 1899–1900 will be Edouard Naville, of Geneva, the well-known Egyptologist.

JOHN P. PETERS,
C. H. TOY,
MORRIS JASTROW, JR.,
} *Committee on Publication.*

October, 1899.

CONTENTS.

LECTURE I. ORIGIN OF THE YAHWEH-RELIGION.

PAGE

Israel's abode in Egypt—Its historical reality is to be maintained, in spite of certain difficulties—The Amarna tablets and the Merneptah inscription—The rescue of Israel by Yahweh—Statement in Old Testament that Israel before this did not know Yahweh—Yahweh the god of the Kenites who dwelt in tents at Sinai—The covenant of Yahweh with Israel was at the same time a covenant of Israel with the Kenites and the acceptance of their religion—Why did Israel accept the Yahweh-religion ?—Because the warrior god, who revealed himself in storm, could and did rescue them from Egypt—How could the Kenite nature-religion become ethical?—Rebuttal of former explanations, and suggestion of a new explanation. 1–38

LECTURE II. YAHWEH AND HIS RIVALS.

Reality of Israel's Baal-worship after the entrance into Canaan—Testimony of the historical and Prophetical books—Testimony of the three annual festivals of Yahweh according to the oldest cultic law—Testimony of the Rechabites and of Hosea—*Necessity* of Israel's Baal-worship—Fragmentary character of the conquest of Canaan ; the Israelites at first dwell among the Canaanites—The Baals long remain the gods of the land, and demand the worship of its inhabitants ; without such worship agriculture, here acquired by Israel, yields no fruit—*Possibility* of the coexistence of Baal-worship and Yahweh-worship—The monotheistic worship of Yahweh can not have been enjoined at Sinai—An-x   Contents

PAGE

tiquity had a special deity for every social circle: Yahweh
was the god of the covenant of the tribes—along with him
in Israel were household gods, sex gods, tribal gods, and
there are traces of astral cults—In Canaan, in addition,
came, in the various districts, the worship of the Baals as
the owners of the soil and the bestowers of the fruits of
the ground—Influence of the new Baal-worship on the Yahweh-worship and on the old Israelitish cults practised in
connection therewith—The original character of the un-
mixed Yahweh-worship.   39–76

LECTURE III. PRIESTS, PROPHETS, KINGS; THE
CHAMPIONS OF YAHWEH.

Yahweh's sole rule in Israel dependent on Israel's sole rule in
Canaan—Rareness of Yahweh-shrines in early times, and
growing need of their multiplication—Micah's sanctuary on
Mount Ephraim and his new Levitical *priest*—Origin and
history of the Tribe of Levi; its claim to priesthood, and
the realisation of the claim —Danger from the Philistines,
Israel's defeats and bondage— Capture and restoration of
the ark of Yahweh—Attitude of penitence in Israel and
its representatives, the *prophets*—Origin and aims of the
Prophetic institution—Saul's connection with the prophets
—The institution of *royalty* tended to establish Yahweh's
sole rule in Israel—Subjection and repression of the remnant of the Canaanites in Israel, and, at the same time, repression of the Baal-cult—Yahweh the Lord of the land
of culture; the Baal-worship becomes a part of his cult—
Justification, in the legends of the patriarchs, of Yahweh-
worship at Baal-shrines—The new sanctuary at Jerusalem,
and its advantages.   77–111

LECTURE IV. THE FOREIGN POWERS AND THE WRIT-
TEN PROPHECY OF THE NORTHERN KINGDOM.

Religious dangers of the monarchy—The alleged idol-worship
of Jeroboam—Solomon's foreign wives—The dynasty of
Omri; Ahab's marriage to Jezebel of Tyre—The worship of
the Tyrian Baal—The bad social effects of the monarchy—

Contents

The revival of Prophecy, and the revolution of Jehu effected by its aid—The writing prophets Amos and Hosea—Amos's belief in Yahweh's absolute power in connection with Yahweh's victory over the Tyrian Baal—Condemnation by Hosea of Jehu's bloody deeds—The reversal, by the Prophets, of their judgment is explicable from the occurrences of their time : not pure ritual, but only moral purity secures Yahweh's favor—Division of the Prophetic Order on this issue—Marks of " true " and " false " prophecy ; rise of written Prophecy out of this distinction—Beginnings of a system of the Yahweh-religion—The question, raised by Amos and Hosea, why Israel was chosen among the nations—The imminent approach of the Great Power, Assyria, regarded by the writing Prophets as an ordination of Yahweh for the punishment of his sinful people—The fall of the Northern Kingdom, and Hosea's prediction of a coming time of favour. 112-141

LECTURE V. THE RELIGION OF YAHWEH IN JUDAH IN CONFLICT WITH THE WORLD-POWER.

Threatening aspect of affairs in Judah after the fall of the Northern Kingdom—Isaiah the Prophet of the Southern Kingdom ; his indebtedness to Amos, and his own peculiar thought—Isaiah and the policy of Judah ; his theory of non-intercourse with foreigners—His rebuff by King Ahaz, and his withdrawal from prophetic activity until the accession of Hezekiah—The religious gain thence resulting—Isaiah's career under Hezekiah—His triumph in the rescue of Jerusalem from Sennacherib—The dogma of the indestructibility of Jerusalem—Its dangers and its permanent value—Manasseh as vassal of Assyria—The period of the predominance of Assyrian culture—The relation of Manasseh's idol-worship to the Yahweh-worship—Hence, also, the religious advantage—Preparation, in the Prophetic and priestly circles, for the reaction—Production of the Book of Deuteronomy—Centralisation of the worship in Jerusalem as a safeguard against the allurements of foreign cults—The reform of Josiah—His enthusiastic faith and his death. 142-180

Contents

LECTURE VI. THE COLLAPSE OF JUDAH, AND THE
BASES OF ITS RE-ESTABLISHMENT.

PAGE

Events up to the capture of Jerusalem—Religious and moral condition of the people—Cultic correctness and secret idol-worship; moral depravation and belief in the indestructibility of Jerusalem—*Jeremiah* and the fall of the State—His life and sufferings—His earlier and later relation to Deuteronomy—His fruitless preaching—His certification as true prophet—His meagre expectations for the future—Severance of the Yahweh-religion from the political organisation of the people—Individualism in religion—*Ezekiel*, the priestly prophet—His denunciatory discourses—His predictions of the restoration of Israel—Sensuous conception of holiness—Complete isolation of Israel from other nations, and of its holy things from things profane within its own area—Rule of the 'priests—Particularism and ritualism—The *Second Isaiah*—His contest against his countrymen's feebleness of faith—Absolute monotheism—Universalism of the Yahweh-religion—The call of Israel to preach Yahweh among the nations—This call explains Israel's suffering—Concluding observations. 181-218

CHRONOLOGICAL TABLE.

	B.C.
Exodus from Egypt	ca. 1250
Invasion of Canaan	before 1200
David becomes king	1000
Division of the kingdom	933
Ahab King of Israel	876–854
Overthrow of the House of Omri	842
The Prophet Amos	ca. 760
" " Hosea	ca. 745
Overthrow of the House of Jehu	743
Call of Isaiah	740
War of Syria and Ephraim against Judah	734–732
Accession of Hezekiah	725
Fall of the Northern Kingdom	722
Siege of Jerusalem by Sennacherib	701
Manasseh King of Judah	696–641
Close of the historical works of J. (from ca. 850) and E. (from ca. 800)	ca. 650
Josiah King of Judah	639–608
Call of Jeremiah	626
Reforms of Josiah, based on Deuteronomy	621
Josiah killed in the battle of Megiddo	604
First capture of Jerusalem by Nebuchadnezzar,	597

Chronological Table

	B.C.
Ezekiel labours as a prophet in Babylonia	593–571
Destruction of Jerusalem; beginning of the Babylonian captivity	586
Deutero-Isaiah	ca. 545
Taking of Babylon by Cyrus	538
Composition of the priestly book of history and law (P.) in Babylonia	ca. 500

PREFACE

IN 1894, Prof. C. H. Toy, of Harvard University, Chairman of the American Committee for Lectures on the History of Religions, on behalf of the Committee, invited me to deliver the fourth series of these lectures, on a subject connected with the history of the religion of old Israel, my immediate predecessor, Prof. T. K. Cheyne, of Oxford, having chosen for his theme " Jewish Religious Life after the Exile." I gladly accepted the honour of this appointment, nor was I long in deciding more definitely upon the subject. Since Professor Cheyne began his lectures with the Babylonian exile, mine must connect with them at that point; since he covered in his course the rest of the Old Testament period, mine must go back to the beginnings. Aside from this, it would have been impossible for me to speak of the early ages of the religion of Yahweh without following it up to its origin.

At first the attempt to traverse so wide a field in six lectures appeared to me excessively difficult. But as I approached the task, it seemed to me that the very constraint which compelled me to be so brief and to confine myself so strictly to the main things could not but be of advantage to the especial aim of the lectures. If the shortest possible line was to be drawn between the starting-point and the goal, it must be all the clearer that this line is a straight one, that the way by which the unique development of the religion of Israel progressed, notwithstanding all apparent deflections and zigzags, really led consistently, necessarily, wisely, and triumphantly upward, and at the point where these lectures stop already opens a vista of the consummation in the Gospel of Jesus Christ. And if I was compelled to abstain almost entirely from referring to the work of analysis and simply to assume its results, it was permitted me to hope that Old Testament scholarship would here present itself not from the negative side, merely as criticism, but as a thoroughly positive work of preserving, restoring, building up, which greatly enriches our conceptions in its field, and causes the masses of material to arrange and articulate themselves in a truly living organism. I might expect in this way to enable intelligent and receptive hearers to gain a distinct view of the subject, undistracted by details, really to increase religious knowledge, and at the same time to awaken and confirm that confidence in our work which is indispensable to us as to all true workmen.

These perhaps too exalted hopes gave me courage for the task and joy in it. In these reflections also I found my guiding principles. I wrote solely for my hearers, such as I imagined them, not for professional scholars and Biblical science. It was not incumbent upon me to trace the history of this branch of learning and scrupulously to assign to each fellow-worker his due; nor to arrive at new results and thus advance learning another step. Almost everything which is contained in these lectures I have for years set before my students in a larger connection, though many things in them may here be published for the first time. So far as it is desirable and possible, I shall hereafter give the grounds of these conclusions more fully in a proper place. But the chief thing for me throughout was the great nexus, the proof of the constancy and consequence of the progress of divine revelation.

A peculiar difficulty, which my predecessors were spared, lay in the necessity of rendering into English lectures which I had written in German. Dr. M. M. Skinner, of Boston, who was at the time studying in Strassburg, was good enough to undertake the translation, and bestowed upon it the utmost care and pains. Prof. B. W. Bacon, of Yale, and Profs. C. H. Toy and D. G. Lyon, of Harvard, very kindly lent their aid in a revision of the translation and in preparing the manuscript for the printers; Prof. G. F. Moore, of Andover, and Dr. J. P. Peters, of New York, have assisted me in the correction of the proofs. I wish in this place to express to them all my sincere thanks. For the fidelity of the translation I myself can vouch.

The lectures were delivered in October, November, and December, 1898, at the University of Chicago, in New Haven (Yale), Cambridge (Harvard), Ithaca (Cornell), at Union Theological Seminary in New York, and the Brooklyn Institute, Brooklyn, finally in Philadelphia (University of Pennsylvania) and Baltimore (Johns Hopkins),— eight times in all. The first and third, connected by a brief synopsis of the second, were given also at the Theological Seminary in Meadville, Pa. I have left the form of the lectures almost unaltered; only a few introductory remarks, and occasional expressions which served the ends of oral delivery, have been omitted. The considerations which were decisive for the lectures as delivered appeared to me to hold good also for the printed form in which they now appear.

Each of the lectures was given in one or more places, as time permitted, in full, as here printed. Whatever new matter attentive hearers in other places may remark, consists only of paragraphs which were passed over or condensed for lack of time. I have introduced such explanations as I deemed necessary in foot-notes; but these also have been kept within as narrow limits as possible. There is no lack, in either English or German, of more extended treatises which will supply what is here wanting; while to the brief outline which is now presented may perhaps be conceded the advantage of novelty.

May it be given to this little book to fill a useful place in the excellent series of which it forms a part, and not to be found unworthy of its predecessors.

KARL BUDDE.

STRASSBURG, August, 1899.

THE RELIGION OF ISRAEL TO THE EXILE.

LECTURE I.

The Origin of the Yahweh-Religion.

THE origin of the Yahweh[1] - religion as the religion of Israel coincides with the origin of the nation itself. The traditional account of these beginnings is found in the Pentateuch, especially in the Book of Exodus. It is a prevalent opinion that the traditions which nations possess regarding their own origin are devoid of all historical value, and that the beginnings of every people are hidden from our

[1] I employ the name " Yahweh " not merely or chiefly because it represents, so far as we can judge, the original pronunciation, but because it is appropriate for our historical investigation. The names "Jehovah" and "the Lord" mean for us the one, eternal God, who does not change; we are here dealing with the early Israelitish conceptions of the Deity—conceptions which, at first crude, grew constantly in purity and elevation till at last, in the progress of revelation, they reached the lofty spirituality of the New Testament. (The word "Jehovah" was made, early in the sixteenth century, by a friar, who was ignorant of the rules of synagogue reading.)

ken by an impenetrable veil. Many think this to be true also of ancient Israel and its religion. There are eminent investigators and authorities who do not venture to use as history anything of the tradition of Israel which goes back beyond the time of David, or, at most, of Saul. For the history of Israel's religion they regard the prophets of the eighth century as the first trustworthy witnesses. For my part, I have more confidence in the sources of Israelitish history and religion. While I recognise the difference between tradition and history, I know, also, that the external form of the tradition is to be carefully distinguished from its content. Tradition in numberless cases clothes genuine history in forms which, at first sight, appear to deserve no confidence at all. The task of the true historian is, first of all, to understand the tradition. When it is correctly understood he will not throw it away, but will make use of it in the proper sense and in the proper place. In this way tradition is transformed into history.[1]

[1] In all fields of historical investigation three stages have succeeded one another in regular order. In the first, tradition is regarded as equivalent to history, and its entire content is accepted on trust without applying to it the test of possibility. In the second, this test is applied; and having convinced themselves that things cannot really have happened as they are reported, men reject tradition as pure fiction; they dispense with its aid, and set in with their historical narrative at the point where manifestly trustworthy sources be-

Thus treated, the Biblical tradition, even of the oldest times, has proved itself to me to be, in its main features, trustworthy—I speak of the history of Israel as a nation, not of the stories of primeval and patriarchal times in Genesis. The thread may become in many places very thin, but it never wholly breaks off; and I venture to hope that I shall succeed in laying before you, in close and uninterrupted dependence on the tradition, a coherent outline of the religion of ancient Israel, as it was progressively ennobled and deepened—a picture self-corroborated by the inner witness of truth.

It is needless to say that to this end I shall make use of the aids afforded by the Biblical investigation, archæology, and comparative history of religion of our day. I cannot give full proof, in the short space at my disposal, of all that I adduce; but an illustrative hint shall never be wanting.

Let us enter on our theme. The cradle of Israel's national existence is located by the tradition in Egypt. Joseph was sold thither and there found

gin. In the third stage only do they take the pains to bring out by skilful questioning the secrets of tradition, to learn to understand it aright, and thus recover from tradition its historical nucleus. The treatment of Greek and Roman history may be cited as a striking illustration of this process. In the history of Israel also, the proper attitude in our time is neither the first nor the second of these stages, but the third.

his fortune. His father Jacob's large family, some seventy souls, followed him later,—a family, not a nation. But Israel came up out of Egypt a nation. Its deliverer and leader was Moses. On Mount Sinai, or Horeb, in the steppe whither he had fled, he had received his call, and the name of the God who called him, who from that time on remained forever the God of Israel, is Yahweh.

No Egyptian monument testifies to this exodus of Israel from Egypt. But if it is historical, it cannot well be dated in any other than the thirteenth century before Christ, somewhere about 1250; for the Israelites had to render forced service at the building of the two cities, Pithom and Ramses.[1] Now the former of these has been laid bare in our days, and at the same time decisive proof has been discovered that it was founded by Ramses II., the Great (the same Pharaoh whose name is borne by the second city), that is, between 1300 and 1250 B.C.[2] Moreover, Ramses II. was the last Pharaoh who swept through Palestine with his armies and held it under firm control. It was not until after his time that Canaan remained for several centuries free from great invasions. It was only during this period,

---

[1] *Cf.* Ex. i. 11.
[2] The discoverer is Ed. Naville; see *The Store City of Pithom and the Route of the Exodus*, Egypt Exploration Fund, 1885.

The Origin of the Yahweh-Religion

then, so far as we can see, that it would have been possible for Israel to gain a firm footing in the land and to assert its nationality over against the older inhabitants. So science has been driven to recognise in Ramses II. the Pharaoh of the oppression, and in his son, Merneptah I., the Pharaoh of the Exodus.

But the most recent discoveries seem to raise a protest against these results. Twelve years ago, a find was made at Tell-el-Amarna in Middle Egypt, which cast an unexpected light on the history and civilisation of Western Asia in the second millennium before Christ. Among other things found at the excavation of the capital of the heretical King Amenophis IV., built about 1400 B.C., were the royal archives, on the whole in a good state of preservation.[1] Among the three hundred or so of these documents (which are in the form of clay tablets) are a large number of letters from petty Canaanite city-kings who, strange to say, make use of the Babylonian language and script in correspondence with their suzerain, the king of Egypt; and among the rest are seven letters from Abd-ḥiba of Jerusalem.[2]

[1] The best publication of this find is by H. Winckler in vol. v. of Schrader's *Keilinschriftliche Bibliothek*. [See also Petrie.]

[2] By the form *Urusalim* they give us the proof that the old name of the city was not *Jebus* or *Shalem*, as late passages of the O. T. (Judg. xix. 10 *f.*; 1 Chron. xi. 4 *f.*; Gen. xix. 18) would have it.

All these letters from Jerusalem implore the speedy aid of the Pharaoh against the warlike people of the Ḥabiri, who have invaded Canaan and threaten to wrest the land from the power of Egypt. Most of the other letters from Canaan and Phœnicia report similar dangers. Although the name of the assailants in these latter documents is different, it is thought permissible, owing to peculiarities of the Babylonian cuneiform writing, to recognise even here the same people, the Ḥabiri. And the most successful of the decipherers of these difficult records, together with other specialists, compares this name with the name ʽIbri, " Hebrews," by which the Israelites are designated in the Old Testament by other peoples, especially by the Philistines and the Canaanites.[1] His conclusion is this: Israel's conquest of Canaan by force of arms and settlement there was not in 1250 B.C., but as early as 1400, long before Ramses the Great; the whole story of the Egyptian sojourn [2] and the Exodus under

[1] *Cf.* H. Winckler, *Geschichte Israels in Einzeldarstellungen*, Teil I. 1895, p. 18 *ff.*

[2] It must be remarked that not all who identify the Ḥabiri with Israel assent to this inference. Hommel has recently expressed the opinion that Amenophis II. (*ca.* 1461–1436 B.C.) is the Pharaoh of the Exodus. [See the *Expository Times*, Feb., 1899, p. 210 *f.*, March, p. 278.] On the other hand, it is well known that the historical character of the sojourn in Egypt was repeatedly questioned before the discovery of the Tell-el-Amarna letters.

Moses is a legend and nothing more. And this view seemed to receive still further support in the year 1896, when a monument was found in the necropolis of Thebes, on which King Merneptah I., the very " Pharaoh of the Exodus" of whom we have spoken, commemorates his victories in hieroglyphic writing. Among the conquered peoples and cities appears, for the first time in an Egyptian inscription, the name of Israel, and, what is more, as many of the best informed think, in such a way as to show that the people must then have been already settled in Canaan. So, according to this also, the entrance into Canaan would have to be set at a considerably earlier date, and the sojourn in Egypt could hardly be regarded as historical.

But in both of these instances it has happened as it so often does in the case of new finds. In the first excitement and joy of the discovery, investigators have far overshot the mark. In the first place, the mention of Israel on the Merneptah-stone is so indefinite, and the abode of the people at that time is so uncertain, that the most varied possibilities are open. After the departure from Egypt, Israel may have encamped in the neighbouring desert and Merneptah may have had a hostile encounter with them there, which, later, he magnifies into a great victory. Again, it is not impossible that the very exodus of which Israel tells may be represented to us in Merneptah's monument as a victory of the Pharaoh. And even these two suppositions are so far from exhausting the possibilities that it appears advisable, for the present, to draw no conclusions at all from the inscription on the Merneptah-stone.[1] Whether the name Ḥabiri in the Tell-el-Amarna letters is really identical with the Old Testament[2] name "Hebrews" remains extremely uncertain. But even if identical, it still proves nothing. For the term "Hebrews" is not a proper name of Israel. The Israelites never so called themselves.[3] The name signifies "those from the other side," and since the Israelites are so named only by the inhabitants of Canaan, this is to be explained as meaning "those who came from the other side of the Jordan." But in the course of centuries many foreign peoples and tribes invaded Palestine from beyond Jordan. It is, therefore, quite possible that the Canaanites gave this name to various peoples in succession before it became ultimately attached to the Israelites.

[1] *Cf.* on this point the thorough discussion of the inscription by A. Wiedemann, "La Stèle d'Israel et sa Valeur Historique." *Le Muséon*, Louvain, xviii., pp. 89–107.

[2] The identity is denied, among others, by George A. Reisner in the *Journal of Biblical Literature*, xvi., 1897, p. 143 *ff.*

[3] This statement is not contradicted by such passages as Gen. xl. 15; Ex. i. 19; xxi. 2, etc. Compare Stade-Siegfried, *Hebräisches Wörterbuch*, p. 480.

Did not the ancient Germans designate all foreign-speaking peoples with whom they came into contact toward the south or west as "Welsche," whether they dwelt in Italy or Gaul, in Great Britain or in Wallachia at the mouth of the Danube? But grant that the Ḥabiri of the Tell-el-Amarna tablets were really the Israelites, in this sense, that the later Israelites had before formed part of this people; even so, the conclusion that Israel took up its abode in Canaan at that time, that is, as early as 1400, and that the Egyptian sojourn therefore rests on legend, would be hasty and inadmissible. For we do not read in these letters that the Ḥabiri succeeded in establishing themselves in Canaan. In order to render the annoying intruders harmless, the Pharaoh may very well have assigned their boldest tribes pasture-land in the border-districts of Egypt, where they would serve as frontier-guards against peoples of the same stamp.[1] Thus the descendants of these same Ḥabiri, or Hebrews, who meet us under Amenophis IV., might have made brick in Egypt under Ramses II., and have fled from the land under the reign of Merneptah to burst once more into Canaan.

Superior to all attacks and doubts there remains

[1] Compare, for example, the settlement of the Ostrogoths in the Eastern Roman Empire at the beginning of the Teutonic migration.

Israel's own self-consciousness. The Israelites knew that their forefathers had been restored by the help of their God from Egyptian bondage to the freedom of the steppe, and thence led to their permanent abode. The witness of the historical documents to this fact does not stand alone. The earliest prophets presuppose it as an incontestable truth.[1] It is inconceivable that a free people should have stamped on the memory of their ancestors the brand of a disgraceful servitude unless it had a foundation of historical truth. All that can be considered doubtful is whether it was the whole people of Israel that fell under the Egyptian bondage, or Joseph alone (that is to say, the tribes of Ephraim and Manasseh, including Benjamin).[2] This latter view seems very probable, but the reasons cannot here be expounded.[3] The importance of the recent excavations, therefore, does not lie in the fact

[1] Am. ii. 10; iii. 1; ix. 7; cf. v. 25; Hos. ii. 15; viii. 13; ix. 3; xi. 1, 5; xii. 9, 13; xiii. 4.
[2] According to tradition (Gen. xxxv.) Benjamin, the younger brother of Joseph, was born—that is, the tribe came into existence—in Canaan.
[3] It is even possible that certain tribes of the second rank joined themselves to Israel after the settlement in Canaan. This would be true of Asher, if the name "Asher" on Egyptian monuments of the thirteenth century refers to this tribe. (See W. Max Müller, *Asien und Europa nach altägyptischen Denkmälern*, 1893, pp. 236 ff.) The greatest caution is necessary, however, in such identifications; in the case of the supposed Egyptian equivalents of the names Jacob and

that they annihilate the Israelitish tradition, but that they prove its possibility and make the course of events conceivable. The Tell-el-Amarna letters show us, in the first place, that attacks of nomadic tribes were repeatedly made on the civilised land of Canaan, on the Mediterranean Sea, in the second millennium before Christ. They show, further, that Canaan possessed a highly civilised population. We have long known from the Egyptian war reports that the Canaanites understood how to win from the soil wheat, wine, oil, and other valuable products in large quantities, and that they had the precious metals, skilfully wrought weapons, and costly utensils. We now know that they even possessed the art of writing and could carry on a political correspondence with the Court of the Egyptian monarch in a foreign language and script. But these letters prove, finally, that these inhabitants were unable even at that time to offer resistance to the vigorous attacks of powerful desert tribes. For they were rent politically, were lacking in military spirit, and had lost the sense of independence by long subjection.

These are exactly the conditions which we have to assume for the period of Israel's entrance into

---

Joseph (*cf.* W. Max Müller, *l. c.*, pp. 162 *ff.*), only the former exhibits a sufficiently close agreement in the consonants, and even this does not make the matter certain.

Canaan, and we now read Israel's own accounts with other eyes. Egyptian monuments have likewise shown us that it was not unusual to admit nomadic tribes into the pasture-land of the border-districts.[1] Admittance was probably thus granted to Israel also. Powerful Pharaohs, who came later, may have assumed the right to raise levies of forced labourers for any great building operations in this district from among these free sons of the desert, as they certainly raised them—so numerous records inform us—among the home-born.

Thus, if not the condition of slavery, at least the feeling among the Israelites that they had been slaves in Egypt, could easily have arisen. Passing the Egyptian frontier fortifications with official permission, as was the case at the entrance, was a very different thing from passing it against the will of the authorities, as was now necessary if they wished to regain the freedom of the steppe. It is no wonder, therefore, that this event impressed itself indelibly on the memory of the following generations as the act which really gave Israel its existence.

At no period did Israel ever fail to ascribe the honour of this deliverance to its God, Yahweh, and to Him alone. It was He who called the fugitive

---

[1] *Cf.* W. Max Müller, *l. c.*, pp. 35 *ff.*, 135 ; though it must be admitted that neither instance exactly corresponds to the case of Israel.

Moses to his divine mission, sending him back to his
brethren in Egypt. It was He who accredited him
by miracles, and who wrung from the inconstant
Pharaoh, by heavy plagues, permission for Israel to
depart. "With a strong right hand and an outstretched arm," He guarded Israel. He caused it to
pass dry-shod through the Red Sea, overwhelming
the army of the Egyptians in its floods. It has not
yet become a strange thing, even to us, that a people should give its god the honour of such deeds,
and no one will find in such a disposition a proof of
incredibility. The story could not fail, therefore, to
bear the stamp of miracle, even if it had been written
down directly after the event. But the later ecclesiastical tradition of both the Jewish and of the Christian churches is very much in error when it claims
that Moses himself wrote the account of these
events. On the contrary, the older written accounts
which are worked up in these books were first set
down, in the form exhibited in their surviving fragments, four or five centuries after him.[1] It is needless
to say, in the case of an ancient people of this sort,
that all individual features of the tradition had, by
this time, completely taken on the impress of
miracle. That which is really astonishing and per-

[1] See S. R. Driver, *Introduction to the Literature of the Old Testament*, or any recent critical work on the same subject.

plexing about it lies in a quarter other than that in which it is usually sought; namely, the tradition claims that it was *not* Israel's *own* God who performed these great deeds, but a God up to that time completely unknown to the Israelites, whose name, even, they then learned for the first time. It was only through the deliverance from Egypt that He won Israel as His people and laid it under the obligation thereafter ever to worship Him.

The narrative of this period in the Book of Exodus is made up from three written accounts. In two of these, the documents called E and P in the critical analysis, Moses himself at the moment of his call does not know the name of the God who sends him back to his brethren in Egypt. In the earlier document E (Ex. iii. 13 *f.*) he asks directly: "Now when I come unto the children of Israel and say unto them, 'The God of your fathers has sent me unto you,' and they ask me, 'What is His name?' what shall I say unto them?" Thereupon, God discloses to him His name Yahweh.[1] The late document P does not think it proper that questions should be addressed by men to the Deity, and substitutes simple revelation (Ex. vi. 2 *ff.*): "I am

---

[1] Read in v. 14b יהוה instead of אהיה, an absolutely necessary emendation, because the third person of the verb can agree only with the subject in the third person, and not in the first.

Yahweh "; thus God announces Himself to Moses. But this is far from being a sufficient explanation for Moses, as it must have been if Yahweh had been Israel's God before this time. On the contrary, the God who is revealing Himself continues: "I appeared unto Abraham, Isaac, and Jacob as God Almighty (*El Shaddai*), but by My name Yahweh I did not make Myself known to them." Therefore the people of Israel, who are languishing in Egypt, have not known Yahweh at all up to this time. On the contrary, they worship idols, as one of these two documents expressly states.¹ Only the patriarchs, the tribal ancestors of Israel, had worshipped Him in times long past, and they without knowing His name. How important a matter this is for both documents appears from the fact that they make use here of the name Yahweh for the first time in their whole narrative, from the creation of the world and the time of the patriarchs on. In all previous passages they speak only of God, or God Almighty. Now the name makes the person, not only among men but also among gods, so long as men believe in a plurality of gods. If, then, the name is new, the god himself is also new. Conversely, to worship a god without giving him a name other than the generic term "God," as

¹ E, in Josh. xxiv. 14.

we do, presupposes the knowledge, which we actually have, that there is only one true God of heaven and earth. It was only a later age, shocked at the idea that the worship of the true God had not always been native to Israel, that ascribed this very advanced knowledge to the patriarchs in primeval times. Still, we cannot wonder that this has been done. For the patriarchs are, in reality, nothing more than the ideal reflection of the nation Israel thrown back into the past,—Israel as it should have been in hoary antiquity. No nation knows the actual father from whom it takes its origin; for nations never arise by derivation from the same father, but by the aggregation of clans and tribes. The realisation of these facts, to be sure, deprives the whole story of the patriarchs of historicity in the narrower sense, but not of historical value, still less of inner worth and psychological truth. It would carry us too far to prove these statements in detail. But it may unhesitatingly be affirmed that they are not the invention of a frivolous, novelty-loving, superficial pseudo-science, but the product of mature reflection and repeated testing. We shall return to the question how the stories of the patriarchs arose in Lecture III. So only one fact remains from this whole tradition, namely, that the God who led Israel out of Egypt had been a stranger to it up to that time. That the forefathers had known Him under this or that name is a palliating addition of the philosophising historian.

Who, then, was Yahweh? whose God?—another question which belief that rests in the letter does not even allow to be propounded. He was, of course, it is sometimes answered, the true, the only true God, the omniscient, omnipotent, omnipresent God, who sought Moses just where He found him and would have found him on any spot; and *because* this true God is named Yahweh, He could disclose no other name to Moses. But this statement can be refuted by the letter of the narrative itself. For when Yahweh appears to Moses in the burning bush, His first command is: "Draw not nigh hither; put off thy shoes from off thy feet for the place whereon thou standest is holy ground" (Ex. iii. 4 *f.*) —holy ground because Yahweh dwells there. For it is the "mountain of God" to which Moses has driven his sheep (Ex. iii.), the same "mountain of God," Horeb or Sinai, on which Yahweh later sits throned in thick cloud at the giving of the law, and on which Moses passes forty days alone with Him in order to receive His commandments. And Israel's new God continues to be connected with this spot in the mind of His people. For when the Israelites are about to depart from Sinai and set out on their wanderings, the question is anxiously asked again and again whether their new and mighty God will accompany them. After long negotiation they are compelled to be satisfied with the concession that the Angel of Yahweh will go with them, while Yahweh Himself remains in His home.¹ When, later, Israel becomes settled in Canaan, and under the leadership of Deborah and Barak fights the decisive battle against the Canaanites in the valley of the Kishon, Yahweh must come through the air from His abode on Mount Sinai to give His people the victory (Judges v. 4 *f.*). And, three centuries later, the prophet Elijah makes a pilgrimage to the " mount of God, to Horeb," in order to seek Yahweh in His home (1 Kings xix.).² We have to do therefore, according to Israel's own view, not with the omnipresent, the only God of heaven and earth, but with a God who is local, who dwells just at that spot where Moses finds Him. The question " To whom did this God belong?" is thus justified and at the same time answered. The God of Sinai must have been worshipped by the people which dwelt in His

¹ Ex. xxiii. 20; xxxii. 34; xxxiii. 1-3. The continuation only shows what difficulties this ancient belief occasioned the Israelites in later times.

² This narrative, written much later than Elijah's time, is proof of the long survival of an idea given up at that time by the leading spirits. See Lecture III. But it should not be forgotten that Elijah's case is an exceptional one.

The Origin of the Yahweh-Religion 19

territory, at Sinai. Now Moses is tending the sheep of his father-in-law Jethro, priest of Midian, when he finds God. He cannot have tended the flocks elsewhere than in the pasture-land of the tribe to which his father-in-law belonged and whose chief he probably was. For the steppe is by no means ownerless. Every nomad tribe knows its own district very well, and woe to the tribe which encroaches on the territory of another! Yahweh, therefore, is the God of the tribe to which Moses, on his flight from Egypt, joined himself by marriage; the mountain-God of Horeb, who appears to him and promises him to lead his brethren out of Egypt.

There is by no means any lack of evidence to show that this conclusion is correct. The tribe with which Moses found refuge and into which he married bears elsewhere the name "Kenite."[1] This would seem to be a narrower term, the more comprehensive name being "Midianite"; *i.e.*, the Kenites were a tribe of the Midianites. Now when the Israelites break camp at Sinai, Moses urgently begs his father-in-law, Hobab, to accompany them as guide through the desert (Num. x. 29 *ff.*). He finally yields to these entreaties; he and his tribe enter Canaan with Israel, and, in company with Judah, conquer for themselves a

---
[1] *Cf.*, especially, Judges i. 16.

territory in the extreme south, where they continue their nomadic life (Judges i. 16).

This kindness of the Kenites was remembered with gratitude even under Saul (1 Sam. xv. 6), and David completed the union of the tribe with Judah (1 Sam. xxx. 29; *cf.* xxvii. 10). This would not have been possible if the Kenites had not been, like Israel, Yahweh-worshippers. And in fact, in the Deborah-battle, of which we have already spoken, the Kenite woman Jael wins praise for the highest bravery in the fight for Yahweh (Judges v. 24 *ff.; cf.* iv. 17 *ff.*).

When Jehu, in the year 842 B.C., overthrows and extirpates the royal house of Ahab which had devoted itself to the worship of Baal, we find Jonadab the son of Rechab standing at his side as the strictest zealot for pure Yahweh-worship and a recognised authority in this religion (2 Kings x. 15 *f.*). Even two hundred and fifty years later, at the siege of Jerusalem by Nebuchadnezzar, we meet his descendants the Rechabites as a sect, almost an order, following a strict and very peculiar manner of life. Acting according to the command of their ancestor Jonadab, they hold it impossible to live in conformity with the will of Yahweh, the God of the desert, save by avoiding wine and the practice of agriculture, and by dwelling in tents instead of houses (Jer. xxxv.). And these Rechabites were, as their genealogy teaches us (1 Chron. ii. 55), a branch of the Kenites, the tribe to which the wife of Moses belonged.

It is clear that what we learn of the Kenites from these passages of the most widely separated periods goes far beyond a mere *participation* in the Yahweh religion. On the contrary, everything indicates that they did not adopt the worship of Yahweh from others, but were conscious of being the proper, the genuine, the original worshippers of Yahweh. Of this fact we have further proof of an indirect sort. There exists, as has been already mentioned, a third narrative, besides the two which teach us that Israel first came to know Yahweh at Sinai. It is the oldest and most original Israelite document, and we call it J, that is, the Yahwist, because it makes use quite naïvely of the name Yahweh as the name of the true God from the creation of the world, and, accordingly, puts it in the mouth of Abraham, Isaac, and Jacob. This is to be explained from the home of the document. For, unlike the other two, it comes from the south, from the land of Judah, the land with which the Kenites had closely associated themselves. This is the narrative which knows most about the Kenites, and in fact it is this which relates the Kenite traditions of the olden time. And just because the Kenites did not, like Israel, adopt Yahweh first under Moses, but had worshipped Him as their God from time immemorial, this Judaic history knows nothing different. It sees in the call of Moses only a new revelation of the old God.

The other ancient narrative, E, however, which is derived from the Joseph tribes of the Northern Kingdom, just because Joseph was the real captive in Egypt, cannot forget how events really came to pass. It knows, and therefore bears witness to the fact, that Yahweh was for Israel a new God. It testifies, further, that Moses' alien relatives had worshipped this God before Israel itself. Let us hear the express confirmation of this statement in the narrative of fundamental importance in Exodus xviii. When Jethro, Moses' father-in-law, learns that Yahweh has brought Israel in safety out of Egypt, he goes to meet Moses "at the mountain of God," bringing him his wife and his two sons. And when Moses tells him how everything took place, he is filled with joy and cries out: " Praise be to Yahweh, who hath delivered you out of the power of the Egyptians; now know I that Yahweh is greater than all gods."

This has generally been interpreted to mean that Jethro, the heathen, now recognises the true God in Yahweh, the God of Israel, and does Him homage. The contrary, however, is the fact. He rather gives expression to his proud joy that *his* God, Yahweh,

The Origin of the Yahweh-Religion 23

the God of the Kenites, has proved Himself mightier than all other gods. For it continues: "And Jethro, Moses' father-in-law, brought a burnt offering and sacrifices, and Aaron and all the elders of Israel came to partake of the meal with Moses' father-in-law before God." "God" is here Yahweh, for this is the document which has constantly used the name "God" up to this point and continues even farther to prefer it. Only once, in the words cited above, it was obliged to use the name Yahweh in order to distinguish Him from other gods, but now it returns to its old habit. Besides, the representatives of all Israel could not take part in the worship of another god. The meal which is eaten before Him is the holy sacrificial meal, which was held at every communal offering, at every bloody sacrifice of the olden time.[1] This sacrifice, however, is not performed by Aaron, nor by Moses, but by the Kenite. *He*, therefore, is the priest of Yahweh, and we now know how we are to understand his title "the priest of Midian." He is the priest of the God Yahweh among the Midianites, or more exactly the Kenites, who serve this God. It is not, therefore, Jethro, who turns to a new God, but Israel, in the persons of Aaron and all the elders of the people, who here for the first time take part in a solemn Yahweh

[1] See, *e. g.*, 1 Sam. i., ii., ix.

sacrifice. This explains, further, why *they* are named while Moses' name is wanting. As related to the Kenites, enjoying the privileges of their tribe, he has long shared in the Yahweh-worship, and no longer needs to be taken into its fellowship. But Aaron and the elders of Israel need this initiation as representative of the redeemed nation which has vowed its service to Yahweh.

What the prophets and historians of Israel later call "Israel's covenant with Yahweh and Yahweh's with Israel" is here described in a sober, historical narrative, in a form which offers nothing at all wonderful when read in the light of ethnology and the history of religions. Expressed in the language of sober historical narration, this covenant is nothing else than an alliance of Israel with the nomad tribe of the Kenites at Sinai, which had as its self-evident condition the adoption of their religion, Yahweh-worship. However, this alliance is rightly called in the Old Testament tradition a covenant of Israel, not with the Kenites, but with Yahweh. For Israel had made the acquaintance of this God earlier than that of the desert tribe which served Him. It had been won to Him by the preaching of Moses in Egypt, and had vowed to dedicate itself to His service before it met the Kenites. We must recognise, therefore, as a fact historically well attested and

The Origin of the Yahweh-Religion 25

supported by many later witnesses, that Israel, simultaneously with its exodus from Egypt and the beginning of its history as a distinct nation, turned to a new religion, the worship of Yahweh, the mountain-God of the Kenites, at Sinai.[1] This is the oldest known example of transition, or conversion, of a people to another religion.[2] Let us consider, in the first place, what were the reasons for this transition at that time, and, secondly, what germs were slumbering therein which would only develop in the future.

The Israel of that time had but one desire and one aim, deliverance from bondage in Egypt. If it became converted to the new God, Yahweh, it took this step because it gave credence to Moses' preaching that this God was able and willing to grant its

[1] All the real or supposititious evidence of the occurrence of the divine name Yahweh among other peoples or in other regions cannot in the least alter this result. Israel became acquainted with Yahweh from this people, in this place, at this time, and was always convinced that it shared the possession of Yahweh with no other. Whether this was an error or not, in any case the religion of Yahweh had in Israel alone and nowhere else the history with which we are here concerned. Through these events the Yahweh of Israel became from this time forth altogether different from what He was in any other nation, even if it should be possible to trace the earlier history of this God among different peoples. We await, therefore, the fuller proof of this without any apprehension that it may unsettle our fundamental position.

[2] The second lecture will show how this conversion should be understood.

wish. This conviction had ripened first in Moses' own bosom. It had unfolded itself to him in the solitude of the steppe, among the flocks, where Mohammed also received his revelations. It is of no real consequence to determine by what means Moses received the revelations which transformed him into the enthusiastic apostle of this God of mountain and desert. But we have every reason to assume that the oral tradition of centuries has given here, as elsewhere, a more and more objective character to the experience. Enough that Moses and the people which believed him attributed to the mountain God of Sinai the power to perform great and warlike deeds, and at the same time the will to make use of this power in Israel's behalf. And they were not mistaken; for under His standard the deliverance from the Egyptian yoke was actually accomplished. And Yahweh proved Himself a wargod even further. Whenever camp was broken, the following words were sung to the portable sanctuary, the Ark of Yahweh, which accompanied Israel henceforward through the desert, and in which, according to the belief of the people, Yahweh miraculously dwelt: "Rise, Yahweh, that Thine enemies may be scattered as dust, and that they that hate Thee may flee before Thy face" (Num. x. 35). In point of fact, Israel does overcome all foes, conquers the land east of the Jordan, and presses victoriously into Canaan. When, later, they are defeated, for the first time, by the Philistines, they have the Ark of the Covenant brought into the camp. The Philistines themselves are seized with terror at this procedure: "Their God is come into the camp. Woe unto us! Who shall deliver us from this terrible God who smote the Egyptians?" (1 Sam. iv. 7 *f.*). The Ark of the Covenant still enters the field as the best ally even under David (2 Sam. xi. 11; xv. 24 *ff.*). The armies of Israel are Yahweh's armies (1 Sam. xvii. 26 *et al.*); its wars the wars of Yahweh (1 Sam. xxv. 28 *et al.*). In short, Yahweh remains for centuries a war-god above all else for ancient Israel.

And this is conceivable enough; for Yahweh wields the most terrible of weapons, the lightning. He appears in the storm at the giving of the law on Sinai (Ex. xix.). He rides on the storm to the Deborah battle (Judges v. 4 *f.*). He reveals Himself in the storm to Elijah on Horeb (1 Kings xix. 11 *ff.*) after having consumed by His lightning Elijah's sacrifice on Carmel (1 Kings xviii. 38). Poetic descriptions also picture Him as revealing Himself in the storm (for example, Psalm xviii. and Habakkuk iii.). Akin to these are the representations of the burning bush seen by Moses at his call, and the pillar of fire and smoke which accompanied the march of Israel through the wilderness. The lightning is called the "fire of Yahweh" and "Yahweh's arrow"; the thunder "Yahweh's voice." The rainbow in the clouds is Yahweh's bow, with which He has shot His arrows, the lightning-flashes, and which he now lays mercifully aside. Yahweh's rule over the storm is explained by his dwelling on Sinai. For the storms gather round the peaks of the mountains south of Palestine. They are at home there, whereas Palestine itself is a land where storms are few. What wonder, then, that the joyful conviction dawned on Moses, when a fugitive in the desert, that the mountain God who sat there enthroned over the storm-clouds was the one to deliver his people out of the power of the Egyptians!

What Israel's transition to Yahweh-worship signified at that time is, therefore, apparent. Israel needed a God mighty in war, and found Him here. So Yahweh remained henceforth, after the entrance into Canaan as well as before, the national God of united Israel, from whom martial aid, above all, was expected in national crises.[1]

But what relation does this God bear to the God in whose name the prophets preach—the God of justice and righteousness, of moral purity and holi-

---

[1] *Cf.*, besides the passages cited before, Judges vi. 11 *ff.*; xiii. 2 *ff.*; 1 Sam. xi. 6; 2 Sam. v. 24, etc.

ness, of mercy and love—the God who rejects His own people and gives victory to the heathen because His people has sinned—the God of heaven and earth, who, finally, through the Gospel of Jesus Christ teaches all mankind to call upon Him as Father, to overcome the world through faith in Him, and to be certain of everlasting bliss in His Kingdom? There we found the mountain God of a nomad tribe, bound to the soil, revealing Himself in the storm, the champion of His own people against all enemies: here we have to do with the highest conception of God which the world knows, with the God of an ethical, universal religion, beside whom there is no other. The name has remained the same; its content has become wholly different. How is this to be explained?

The germ of this development has been rightly sought in the earliest form of the conception. Only we must go about the search in the right way. In such an enquiry nothing is gained by attempting to discover in the name Yahweh, by the aid of philological derivation and translation, some profound and sublime meaning, be it "the eternal one," "the truly existent," or whatever else has been suggested. The meaning of an ancient proper name is always very difficult to determine, and in the present case there is at least as much to say for the signification "he who overthrows or annihilates" as for the others proposed. But for this, too, an adequate degree of probability is unattainable.

Others have followed the easy road of supposition. It has simply been assumed that the religion of Yahweh, in distinction from other religions, had a deep moral trait, or, to put it more personally, that Moses was gifted with religious genius which qualified him to supply the Yahweh religion with its ethical content, so that no more remained for the prophets than to bring this to full understanding and recognition. Nothing is explained by such assumptions. For one thing is certain from the outset: Yahweh, when accepted by Israel, was the God of a rude nomad tribe in the desert. The primitive worshippers of Yahweh, the Kenite Rechabites, even in later times still held agriculture and a settled life to be incompatible with faithfulness to Yahweh. And Israel, too, which in all probability then first arose as a nation through the fusion of a number of related tribes, was a nomad people. True, it had come into external contact with a higher civilisation in Egypt, but it had refused with repugnance to adopt it. If the new religion to which the Israelites turned had not corresponded to the stage of civilisation which they had reached, men might have accepted it externally, but it would never have maintained itself so tenaciously in the face of all other influences. And what we observe with certainty in the utterances of Yahweh and in the religious customs of the oldest period corresponds only too well to the picture given us by historical research, of the religions of the Semitic nomad tribes.[1] The sacred ban by which conquered cities with all their living beings were devoted to destruction, the slaughter of human beings at sacred spots, animal sacrifices at which the entire animal, wholly or half raw, was devoured, without leaving a remnant, between sunset and sunrise,—these phenomena and many others of the same kind harmonise but ill with an aspiring, ethical religion.

We are further referred to the legislation of Moses, under whose name a complete and minute code has been transmitted to us, comprising civil and criminal, ceremonial and ecclesiastical, moral and social law in varying compass. This legislation, however, cannot have come from Moses. For even in its oldest strata it presupposes a settled, agricultural life, and Israel did not reach this point until after Moses' death. Such legislation can only have arisen after Israel had lived a long time in the new home, had gained a wide experience on this new stage of civilisation, and, in particular, had become

[1] See W. Robertson Smith, *Religion of the Semites*, 2d ed., 1894.

acquainted with the legal complications and difficulties which this altered mode of life brought with it. It is not at all surprising that this body of laws now passes under Moses' name. For he was the founder and deliverer to whom Israel owed both its national existence and its religion. On this account he came to be looked upon as the only lawgiver for all time. Everything that became a prevailing custom in Israel had to be referred back to Moses in order to be adopted into the written code, for thus only could it receive force as law. For example, the law of booty, which on the unmistakable testimony of the Book of Samuel (1 Sam. xxx. 22 *ff.*) was first introduced by David, now stands in the Book of Numbers (xxxi. 25 *ff.*), without explanation, as Mosaic law.

But many scholars, while relinquishing everything else, have tried to save the Ten Commandments, the "Mosaic" moral law, for these oldest times. Now the Ten Commandments base all their demands on the nature of the God of Israel. If, then, they really did come from this period, it appears that there existed, even in the earliest times, a conception of God so sublime that hardly anything could have remained for the prophets to do. This of itself should suffice to show the impossibility of the Mosaic origin of the Ten Commandments.

But they were, besides, for oldest Israel, both superfluous and impossible. For morality within the limits of a nomad tribe is regulated spontaneously by the feeling of blood-kinship without the need of any written word, and is protected by strict patriarchal discipline. But a universal prohibition reaching beyond the limits of the tribe, of manslaughter or theft, to say nothing of other sins, is simply inconceivable to the nomad.

Confronted on all sides by insurmountable obstacles, some writers, including in particular certain of the most renowned representatives of Biblical scholarship[1] to-day, have taken final refuge in the ancient tradition that Moses administered justice in Yahweh's name, and in the fact that we have many other traces of the delivery of sacred legal decisions in ancient Israel. This tradition exists, it is true. According to Ex. xviii., Jethro, the Kenite, was Moses' experienced teacher in this very science. He advised him how to lighten the load of sacred judgment, which had become too burdensome. If, therefore, so runs the conclusion, Yahweh was the God of law, of justice,—that is, of righteousness,—then the conception of the moral God who demands holiness, as the prophets preach Him, must have developed from this germ. But this is an exceedingly bold

---

[1] Under the leadership of Kuenen and Wellhausen.

step, a true *salto mortale*, which proves only the desperate case of him who resorts to it. For law and morality are two entirely different things. Morality may indeed create law or mould existing law for its own external protection, but the converse is impossible. We must, moreover, bear in mind what was meant by ancient judgment, and how it was accomplished. It served to detect or convict the culprit in case of a crime, to render the decision in case of a dispute over "mine and thine." Both were done by Yahweh, but by what means? Not by moral investigation and instruction, but by an oracular response obtained by means of a sacred lot. Some centuries later this was still the practice,[1] and it is reported to have been so in Moses' time.[2] Yahweh is here the source, not of moral, but simply of intellectual knowledge. He, the God, knows what is hidden from men and communicates His knowledge through the oracle. Moreover, such oracles were delivered not only by Yahweh, but also by the gods of the heathen, the gods of the Moabites and Ammonites, of the Philistines and Aramæans, and all the rest of them. Each people sought judgment from its own god. And yet their religions did not develop into ethical religions. So

---

[1] 1 Sam. xiv. 38 *ff*.
[2] Ex. xxii. 6 *ff*.; *cf*. Josh. vii. 16 *ff*.

far as we know they remained what they were, and sank into the grave with the peoples themselves.

Thus all attempts to find the germ of the ethical development of the Yahweh-religion in the material content of the conception of God as represented by Moses have completely failed. Let us now enquire whether by asking the question "How?" instead of "What?" we cannot reach a better result. *How* did Israel come to its religion? It went over, at Sinai, to a rude nomad religion, a religion which did not stand higher than that of other tribes at the same stage of civilisation. It served henceforth the same God as the tribe of the Kenites to which Moses' wife belonged. But the Latin proverb rightly says, "When two do the same thing it is not the same." For one fundamental difference existed between Israel and the Kenites from the beginning. The latter, like numberless other tribes and peoples, had had their god from time immemorial. But Israel had turned to Him of its own free will, and chosen Him as its God. The Kenites served their god because they knew no better; because he was of their blood-kindred, and had grown up in inseparable union with them; because his worship belonged to the necessary and almost unconscious expression of the life of the people. This was still the case with their remote descendants, the Rechabites of the time of

Jeremiah. But Israel served Yahweh because He had kept His word; because He had won Israel as His possession by an inestimable benefit; because it owed Him gratitude and fidelity in return for this boon, and could ensure its further prosperity only by evidences of such fidelity.

Thus, in the very transition to this new religion, virtues were both awakened in the heart of the people and maintained in continuous watchfulness. If Yahweh-worship itself had no ethical character, this relation to Him had such character, and all future development could spring therefrom. Look about and see how external the worship of the old nature religions generally was,—how carelessly, how familiarly, how defiantly primitive man is accustomed to have intercourse with his hereditary gods![1] But Israel met at Sinai a God unknown to it before. It knew, however, this much of Him from experience, that He was a great and powerful God, who could help if He would. It could adopt His worship only with fear and dread, always in doubt whether it had fathomed the depths of His nature, whether its actions found favour with Yahweh and would be regarded as sufficient proof of fidelity. Whenever things went badly with the people it was far from thinking that Yahweh had not power to help. On the contrary,

[1] See W. Robertson Smith, *Religion of the Semites*, p. 60 *f*.

its conscience awaked each time to the questions: "Wherein have I deserved the displeasure of Yahweh? What must I do to ensure a renewal of His favour and help?" Thus arose a really living force, whose operation tended to the ethical development of Israel's religion.

It depended, to be sure, on the further experiences of Israel whether the effects of this force would be lasting, whether a truly ethical religion would develop from these ethical impulses. Israel might have found at Sinai a comfortable and permanent home; it might peacefully have shared the pasture-lands of the Kenites, and have adopted the old nomad life in all its primitiveness. Had Israel done so, it certainly would have been no longer possible after a few centuries, or even after a less interval of time, to distinguish the newly adopted religion from any other nature-worship. The people of Israel, together with its God, Yahweh, would have sunk into obscurity, like Moab with its Chemosh, like the Philistines with their Dagon, and countless others.

God willed it otherwise. He continued to lead Israel onward through new vicissitudes. He kept that ethical force alive by ever-changing experiences and by tests constantly renewed. Ever and again Israel thought of Yahweh as its helper, and of the obligation of gratitude and fidelity by which alone it could be sure of His help. Thus the demands which in Yahweh's name men imposed upon their own consciences rose slowly but surely. They increased with the nation's advance in civilisation and moral knowledge. Mighty spirits who had themselves sprung from this fermentation, who were themselves actuated and inspired by God, took deep hold in the process, and gave ever new impulses. In the following lectures we shall trace not only their work, but, side by side with it, the wonderful guidance of God. But the germ of this whole development took root at Sinai. *Israel's religion became ethical because it was a religion of choice and not of nature, because it rested on a voluntary decision which established an ethical relation between the people and its God for all time.*

LECTURE II.

Yahweh and His Rivals.

DID Yahweh have rivals? Could there be gods who shared with Him the power over Israel, who with Him were venerated by Israel? If we enquire of the law, it was not possible. The first commandment of the Decalogue runs, "Thou shalt have no other gods beside me," and v. 14 of the Yahwistic Decalogue, Exodus xxxiv., which is probably still older, "Thou shalt not worship any other god." But the existence of the commandment does not prove its observance. In close proximity to this prohibition in Exodus xxxiv. stand most impressive warnings to the Israelites against allowing themselves to be led into idolatry by the peoples whose land Yahweh is to give to Israel as a possession. This warning is repeated again and again in Deuteronomy, and at the end of the book the people are threatened with the severest penalties if they allow themselves to be led astray. This does not sound very encouraging when we reflect that these legal portions of the Pentateuch were written, not before the entrance into Canaan, but many centuries later, when Israel had behind it all the experiences which are represented in these passages as lying in the future. In point of fact, when we consult the historical books we find it stated that Israel disregarded all commandments and threw all warnings to the winds. As soon as the generation which had lived through the deliverance from Egypt was extinct, Israel forsook its God, Yahweh, and served the Baals, the gods of the peoples who dwelt round about (Judges ii. 11 *ff.*). Yahweh reiterates this charge against the people to Samuel (1 Sam. viii. 8); and if we ask the prophets, we are told by Ezekiel (ch. xx.) that Israel never ceased to serve idols in Egypt, in the wilderness, and in the Promised Land which Yahweh gave it as a possession. Only by fresh chastisements, alternating with ever-recurring favours, did Yahweh succeed in calling the people back to Him and keeping it by Him, otherwise it would have been irretrievably lost from the very beginning.

Still, if the course of events had actually been that depicted in these passages, we should hardly have reason to occupy ourselves minutely with Yahweh's rivals. For if the fact was that Yahweh was forsaken for the service of other gods, and the rival gods were in turn forsaken for the service of Yahweh, they would not have exercised a lasting influence on Israel. The course of events would have been that it threw these gods aside as one casts off a garment, and with them everything that pertained to their worship; that the people recognised its sin, and from this time on exercised all the greater diligence to serve Yahweh purely, till at last the time came when the unadulterated Yahweh-worship, just as Moses had established it, unendangered by external influences, attained undivided sway.

But the actual course of events was different. The Yahweh-worship of a later period was no longer the same that Israel had adopted from the Kenites in the wilderness, and the worship of "other gods" had materially contributed to the change. Yahweh had not expelled and annihilated them, but had made them subject; He had divested them of their personality by absorbing them into His own person. To be sure, neither the Law, nor the historical narratives, nor the prophets say a word of all this, and yet it can be proved, and all the sources mentioned must yield us their share of proof.

The nature of a god who belongs not to imagination but to actual life is determined by the worship which is paid him. Now the fundamental ritual requirement which Yahweh makes of Israel in Exodus xxiii. and Exodus xxxiv. is the celebration of three feasts in the course of the year. "Three times shalt thou keep a feast unto Me in the year. The feast of unleavened bread shalt thou keep. Seven days shalt thou eat unleavened bread, as I commanded thee, at the time appointed in the month of ripe ears . . . ; *and* the feast of the harvest, the first-fruits of thy produce which thou sowest in the field ; *and* the feast of the ingathering at the end of the year, when thou gatherest in thy produce out of the fields." All these are agricultural feasts—that of the first ripe ears, substantially the barley-harvest ; that at the gathering in of the grain, wheat-harvest, seven weeks later, and that of the vintage and fruit-harvest in autumn. In the later legislation also, in Deuteronomy xvi., Leviticus xxiii., and Numbers xxviii., these feasts stand out clearly as agricultural thanksgiving days.

But what has Yahweh to do with agriculture? Was He not the God of the steppe, of the tent-dwelling nomad tribes? Must not everything which originally belonged to His worship find its origin and place in the life of the nomad? It will be objected that Yahweh had become known as the mighty God who was superior even to the Egyptians; that the firm conviction was cherished that He would become master of the new land which He purposed to give to Israel; that, accordingly, it was the most natural thing in the world that He should adapt His laws and His worship to the conditions of this new land, even though in the wilderness there could be as yet no offerings of firstling sheaves or loaves. Whether Israel in the wilderness was already greatly preoccupied with its mode of life in Canaan, whether laws for the future like these are probable, we may leave undecided. But if Yahweh disposes in advance of the fruits of agriculture in the Promised Land, He must feel Himself lord of the land, He must permeate and bless the soil which yields these fruits. Was this Israel's conviction when it entered Canaan? For a long time thereafter it surely was not; for we have seen that Yahweh was not thought of as dwelling in Canaan, but now, no less than before, on Sinai in the steppe. Only in exceptional cases did He come from His mountain home, in human form, as a wanderer, or through the air in the storm-blast. Even at a late period men still sought Him at Horeb-Sinai when they wished to be sure of finding Him (1 Kings xix.).

But this negative evidence is re-enforced by a positive proof. Not everyone in Israel was convinced that these feasts belonged to Yahweh, not all can have taken part in them. I refer to the Rechabites, the descendants of Jonadab ben Rechab, with whom Jeremiah came into contact during the siege of Jerusalem, B.C. 597 (Jer. xxxv.). For two hundred and fifty years they had strictly followed the injunction of their ancestor to drink no wine, to sow no seed, to possess neither vineyards nor fields, to build no house nor dwell in one. The promise which is made them, on these conditions, is that they shall live long in the land where they are now sojourners. We perceive that Jeremiah does not share their convictions. He treats all these regulations simply as ordinances of their ancestor, and not as commandments of Yahweh binding on all. This ancestor, however, is well known to us. We know from 2 Kings x. that he was a zealot for pure and simple Yahweh-worship, who stood at Jehu's side when he extirpated Baal-worship in Israel. Jonadab had, therefore, certainly issued his ordinances in Yahweh's name. He must have believed as firmly that their observance was the only pure and strict Yahweh-worship as he did that only Yahweh was capable of fulfilling the accompanying promise. Can it be supposed that these Rechabites held to the prescriptions of the Law regarding those three feasts; that in the month Abib they offered the first-fruits of the sheaves and for seven days ate unleavened bread; that at Pentecost they celebrated the feast of the completion of the grain-harvest, and in the autumn the feast of the vintage, or, as it is also called, the feast of the threshing-floor and the winepress? This is inconceivable. Wine they abhorred, bread they may not have disdained when they happened to procure it by exchange, but they can never have lent themselves to the celebration of feasts for the successful issue of labours which in the name of their God were strictly forbidden them. They certainly must have asserted that these festivals did not belong to Yahweh,—that they were a foreign worship. Who knows whether they did not brand them as idolatry, as Doctor Martin Luther and John Knox did the Romish mass? Nay, there was a time when they would not have stood alone in this. Thus, the prophet Hosea, who lived a hundred years after Jonadab and more than a hundred years before Jeremiah, makes the Israel of his time say, " I must go after my lovers that give me my bread and my water, my wool and my flax, mine oil and my drink"—that is, my wine (Heb. text ii. 7, Eng. ii. 5). But these lovers are, according to v. 14 *f.*, the Baals, the gods of Canaan; going after them means nothing else than practising idolatry. Now if the Israelites thought themselves indebted to these gods for the corn and all other products of the land, it must surely have been in their honour, and not in Yahweh's, that they celebrated the feasts which expressed their thanks.

This does not mean that the Feast of Unleavened Bread, the Feast of Pentecost, and the Feast of Tabernacles were as yet not Yahweh-feasts at all, and that, accordingly, the laws regarding feasts in Exodus xxiii. and xxxiv. had in Hosea's time not as yet come into existence. On the contrary, Yahweh instructs His people through the mouth of the prophet (v. 10), that all these blessings came not from the Baals, but from Him, and that, accordingly, the worship which they were paying these gods belonged by right to Him. Still, a large circle in Israel were certainly conscious, even then, that they celebrated these three great feasts in honour not of Yahweh, but of the Baal; and if the prophets had to assert the contrary as something new, the others had ancient tradition in support of their view. A hundred years earlier, when Jonadab ben Rechab lived, a much more numerous circle must have shared this conviction. He forbade his descendants to follow agriculture and wine-growing for the very reason that these, according to his conviction, inevitably led to idolatry.

But even Hosea himself knows that these feasts do not belong to the most ancient Yahweh-worship, for he declares that the ultimate measure for converting and reforming unfaithful Israel will be to lead it back into the wilderness. There, where

Israel has neither vine nor fig-tree, it shall learn again to serve Yahweh as in the days of its youth, and as in the day when it came up out of the land of Egypt (v. 16 *f.*).[1] That these three harvest feasts could not be celebrated in the desert is obvious. It is in this sense that Hosea's predecessor, Amos, enquires, " Did ye bring unto me sacrifice and offering forty years in the wilderness, O house of Israel?"[2] Hosea's inference is not only that Yahweh can be worshipped without these feasts, but also that His worship is purer without them, that there is less danger of sin when they are not celebrated.

Accordingly, all the witnesses are fundamentally agreed: the blind mass of the people, who serve the Baalim because they believe themselves indebted to them, and not to Yahweh, for the blessings of agriculture; the sectarian Puritans, who abhor agriculture because they are convinced that it will lead them to idolatry; the prophet, who knows that the desert guarantees a purer worship of Yahweh. Under such circumstances the question how such new influences could creep into Yahweh-worship becomes extremely important. Its answer must be sought in Israel's experiences.

[1] *Cf. The New World*, Boston, December, 1895, p. 733 *ff.* These verses are by no means to be struck out, with Nowack, but simply to be emended in the manner I have proposed.

[2] Am. v. 25.

From the wilderness where it had found its God Yahweh, Israel invaded a land of high civilisation. In the land of Canaan, between the Jordan and the Mediterranean, it found its proper home. Only a few tribes on the east of the Jordan acted as intermediaries between Israel on the one hand and its remoter kindred, Moab, Ammon, and the tribes of the steppe on the other hand. But here again, reality was quite different from theory. According to the theory, all Canaan without exception was conquered in three campaigns by united Israel under the lead of Joshua, and divided up among the tribes. The previous inhabitants were pitilessly exterminated, and Joshua exacted once more from the people assembled at Shechem the sacred promise to serve Yahweh alone. So reads the Book of Joshua, in admirable harmony with the promises of Deuteronomy. We learn the reality in the first chapter of Judges, and the most important statements of this chapter receive confirmation from a number of passages scattered through the Book of Joshua.[1] According to these, the campaigns were not conducted by all Israel, but, from Jericho as a centre, each group of tribes sought to conquer its own district by its own efforts. The result was anything but complete and satisfactory.

[1] Josh. xiii. 13; xv. 13-19; v. 63; xvi. 10; xvii. 14-18; xix. 47. See K. Budde, *Die Bücher Richter und Samuel*, 1890, pp. 1-89.

Yahweh and His Rivals

True, all the groups succeeded in climbing the mountain passes and in getting a foothold on the highlands, but not one is able to conquer its entire district. So the national unity of Israel, won in the desert, was lost again.

The kernel of the Israelites rescued from Egyptian bondage, that is, the House of Joseph, consisting of Ephraim and Manasseh and the young tribe of Benjamin on the south, established themselves in the centre of the land later called Samaria, in the hill-country of Ephraim. But they were unable to conquer the plain of Sharon south of Carmel and so reach the seacoast, and were equally unsuccessful against the plain of Jezreel in the north, as well as against the southern slope of the mountain-range of Ephraim, with the broad valleys which lead up to Jerusalem from the coast. "They could not drive out the Canaanites in the plain," says Judges i. 19, "for they had chariots of iron." They were superior to the Israelites in the art of war; their weapons were too formidable, their cities too strong. Thus in the north a zone of Canaanite territory extended from the coast by Acco to the Jordan, protected by fortified cities, Bethshan near the Jordan, Ibleam, Taanach, and Megiddo, in the plain of the Kishon, and Dor at the southern base of Carmel. In the south ran a similar stretch of territory, from Gezer on the extreme spurs of the mountains, through Ajalon and Shaalbim on the one side and Beth-shemesh on the other, up to Jerusalem, the strongest city of Canaan, which maintained its independence down to David's time. These two belts of iron interrupted communication and checked intercourse. Ephraim was cut off on the one side from the northern group of tribes, Issachar, Zebulon, Naphtali, and Asher, and on the other from the tribe of Judah, which, together with Simeon and their non-Israelite allies, the Kenizzites, Kenites, and Jerachmeelites, had conquered a seat for themselves in the mountain country south of Jerusalem and in the steppe land of the Negeb.

Each of these groups was for the time being so occupied with its internal affairs as not to feel the lack of communication with the others. We happen to know from Judges ix. that even the House of Joseph was not able to subdue all the Canaanites in the mountain district, for the city of Shechem, in the very heart of Samaria, nestling among its most fruitful fields, remained independent for a long time after. Of how many other cities this was true we do not know. Judah was fully occupied with the warlike nation of the Philistines in the plain, along the seacoast, and in the hill-country. The little tribe of Dan, on the north-west border of Judah, was even compelled to give up the struggle with the native inhabitants. The liberty-loving minority journeyed forth and sought for itself a new home far up in the north, at the sources of the Jordan (Judges xvii., xviii.); the majority bowed to the foreign yoke. Asher and Naphtali dwelt on the mountains of Galilee, wholly "in the midst of the Canaanites," not with the Canaanites in the midst of them,—according to the laconic but significant change of phrase in Judges i. 32, 33,—split up, in other words, into innumerable fragments, and therefore in the greatest danger of losing their Israelitish nationality and being merged with the Canaanites.

Everywhere, in the long run, treaties inevitably took the place of a state of war. The two peoples settled down peaceably side by side and accepted one another's presence. Of these treaties we have the best example, Shechem excepted, in the compact with the cities of Gibeon, Beeroth, Chephirah, and Kiriath-Jearim, which encircle Jerusalem on the west. Although this treaty is now referred back to Joshua himself (Josh. ix.), it was really made much later.

What were the religious consequences of the conditions thus sketched? The new abodes had been conquered in Yahweh's name and with His help, and we know that neither He nor His worship had been given up. The shrine which had been brought along from Sinai, the Ark of Yahweh, we find again later at Shiloh, in the hill-country of Ephraim, under the guardianship of a priesthood.[1] The Yahweh-worship can never have become extinct at this temple. In Bethel the Angel of Yahweh revealed himself at the very moment of the entrance into Canaan, and the result was that sacrifice was offered to Yahweh there (Judges ii. 1, 5^b).[2] Thus in the House of Joseph the memory of the deliverance from Egypt by Yahweh's hand was kept alive. Judah, on the other hand, won territory on the south which put it in touch with Sinai, the dwelling-place of Yahweh; for its allies pitched their tents in the southern steppes which reached to the mountains of Seir and the abodes of those Kenites who had remained behind. So through the medium of these allies there must have developed and have been perpetuated a primitive Yahwism in which Yahweh was venerated because He was the hereditary god from time immemorial. Matters went worse, no doubt, in the northern third, where Yahweh-worship probably did not obtain a firm seat until the establishment, at a later period,

---

[1] See 1 Sam. i.–iv.; especially iii., iv.
[2] The texts ought to be restored according to the Septuagint; vv. 2–5^a are a later addition; see Budde, *Richter und Samuel*, pp. 20 ff.

through the migration of the Danites, of the new sanctuary at Dan.¹

But in any case, Yahwism could not remain Israel's only worship. In antiquity every land is animated by a god and in a god's possession. If the land consists of waste and uninhabited stretches, spirits and demons are looked for there, erratic, malevolent beings, doubly feared because no one knows how they should be met, nor what they may demand of him who sets foot upon their territory. If, on the other hand, it be a question of inhabited land, of cultivated soil, men know quite well, or can at least find out, what the characteristics of its god are, and by what means his favour may be secured.

Accordingly, whoever comes into a foreign land and wishes to take up his abode there must serve the god or gods of this land. This is assumed as self-evident in the Old Testament also. When David, in his flight, meets Saul, he curses his slanderers, because they have driven him out from a share in the heritage of Yahweh, and have said, "Go, serve other gods" (1 Sam. xxvi. 19). He knows that as soon as he gets into a foreign land he must render to its gods the worship due them; and this requirement he certainly cannot have wholly

---

¹ Judges i. 34; Josh. xix. 42; Judges xvii., xviii. See Budde, *Richter und Samuel*, pp. 15-18, 28-32.

escaped when he lived among the Philistines. After the deportation of the Ten Tribes, the Assyrians plant foreign settlers in North Israel. When these are harassed by wild beasts, they send to Assyria for a Yahweh priest. He teaches them the characteristics of the God of the country, that is, Yahweh, and instructs them how they must serve Him. So thenceforth they serve Yahweh, but, in addition, every one his native gods, and the plague ceases (2 Kings xvii. 25 *ff.*). It may be objected that the historicity of both these narratives rests on very insecure foundations, and that the second, particularly, is very late. So much the better, for it proves all the more conclusively that Israel, even in very late times, held it as self-evident that one should render due honour to the god in whose land he dwelt. *Cujus regio, ejus religio!* this is the ruling principle.

Now the gods of Canaan had indeed been conquered by Yahweh; but they had not been driven out, for Yahweh had not taken up His abode in Canaan. He continued to sit enthroned on Mount Sinai, and His dominion was the steppe. Besides, even if the original inhabitants had been defeated, and many of them doubtless killed, they had not been expelled or exterminated. Part of them lived under Israel in a state of dependence defined by treaty; part remained independent and victorious in the

Yahweh and His Rivals

defence of their possessions. Thus the ancient gods had after all kept their power and possessions, notwithstanding the Israelite invasion. They proved that they were still alive, and demanded service from the invaders. In this light we can readily understand why the later historical theory represents Canaan as completely conquered and all the Canaanites as exterminated; this alone made it logically possible to demand from Israel the exclusive worship of Yahweh.

Moreover, in entering Canaan, Israel not only passed from one land into another, but took the more important step from one plane of civilisation, from one mode of life, into another and a higher. Up to this time the Israelites had been nomads. They had wandered about with their flocks in a definite pasture land, pitching their tents now here, now there, tarrying here a longer, there a shorter time, but nowhere striking root in the soil. The flocks alone had furnished them food, clothing, and shelter. They had asked nothing more of the soil than what they found when they set foot upon it—the verdure which furnished food for their flocks. But the land into which they now entered was an ancient seat of civilisation. Barley and wheat, wine and oil, were raised there in great abundance from very early times. If Israel would live in the narrow quarters which it had wrested from the Canaanites, wedged in as it was among them, then it too must learn the art of agriculture. So Israel accommodated itself to a settled mode of life and to agriculture, and thereby took the most important step which can be taken in the scale of human civilisation. There was much to learn, and in everything the Canaanite neighbour, whether conquered or free, was Israel's teacher.

Now the indispensable operations of agriculture at that time consisted not merely of fertilising, ploughing, sowing, reaping, threshing, pruning of the vines, and whatever else may be reckoned among agricultural pursuits; the worship due to the god who bestowed the blessings of harvest was considered just as necessary as, nay, more important than anything else. After all, there is nothing new in this. Do not we also know the *ora et labora?* But there is an essential difference between our attitude on this point and that of the Israelite in his new home. It is not the earthly blessing that we implore in the first place from our Heavenly Father, and we know that His blessing is not procured by rites of worship. In the olden time men sought the earthly blessing alone, and belief that worship is the means to obtain it was universal, so that no one ever thought of trying to evade this necessity.

We pray to-day to the same God, whether in the Old World or the New, whether we look for His blessing on our crops, or our herds, or our commercial and industrial undertakings, or whatever it may be. The Israelite of the olden time could expect no blessing from his God, Yahweh, upon agriculture, for He was a God of the steppe and had no control over the treasures of the cultivated land.¹ But the god whom the Canaanites venerated, the Baal, that is, the "possessor" of land and soil, had this control. We learn from Hosea of the people's conviction that they must serve him if their labours were to be successful, if they would reap where they had sown. This service Israel learned from its Canaanite teachers. They told the Israelites that all the laborious work of the farmer would be of no avail, if the worship, consisting of such and such rites, were not paid to the Baal. The sun would scorch everything; the mountain torrent would bury the crops under gravel and mire; the seed would choke in the soil; the locusts would eat everything bare; earthquakes would hurl their dwellings to the ground, if men did

¹ W. Robertson Smith (*Religion of the Semites*, pp. 81 *ff.*), utters a just caution against defining the nature of the individual Semitic deities, as though each presided only over a particular class of natural phenomena or moral actions. He emphasises the fact that the ancient worshipper sought and expected from his god everything that he needed. But where peoples stand on the border line between two diverse stages of culture this rule cannot be strictly applied. Conflicts must arise there such as we have depicted ; and only after these have been allayed does the rule again hold good.

not show the Baal the honour due.¹ Anyone who withheld this service—let us suppose, out of fidelity to another god—would be forced by the majority to render it, or be driven out of the community as impious. For his impiety must bring down the divine punishment on many innocent persons, just as surely as all Israel in Joshua vii. must suffer for the theft of Achan alone, or in 1 Samuel xiv. for Jonathan's eating of the honey. Thus Israel was forced to learn the service of Baal as part of the art of agriculture, and, doubtless, also, as chief constituents of this worship, the harvest festivals which later appear as the indispensable obligations of a faithful Yahweh-worshipper.

The results thus reached serve at once to confirm what the historians as well as the prophets assert, namely, that Israel learned to serve Baal in Canaan, and to explain Israel's idolatry, the infidelity to Yahweh of which it became guilty by this new worship. But was it really infidelity to Yahweh? Were the Israelites conscious of such infidelity? Was it not, according to the conviction of Israel, Yahweh Himself who had sent Israel into this land? And had He not expressly refused to enter the new land in His own person? Had He not remained in the wilderness,

¹ *Cf.* Land, "De wording van staat en godsdienst in het oude Israel," in *De Gids*, 1871, No. 10.

leaving the Baal in possession of the land and its gifts? Appearances taught all this, and this was Israel's conviction.

It is, therefore, in the highest degree improbable that Yahweh demanded at Sinai the exclusive veneration of His own godhead. True, this is the unvarying testimony of Old Testament tradition. It is to this day the generally accepted view, and is held even by advanced specialists. But it can hardly be maintained. Not that I would deny that Yahweh was the only God of the nation Israel. As long as the nation Israel has existed Yahweh has been its only God, and as long as it continues to exist He will so remain. But in antiquity there were not only national gods, but also clan, family, and household gods. Every social unit had its special god, nor was any association formed between men which was not dedicated to a special deity and placed under his protection.

When, therefore, Israel, from a number of tribes, became welded together at Sinai into a nation, entering at the same time into alliance with the tribes at Sinai, it was forced to place this new federation under the charge of a special god. This god could not have been before the god of all Israel, for up to this time a united Israel had not existed. But whether it was the god of a part of Israel who came to occupy this position, or, as really happened and could not fail to happen, the god of the Kenites who dwelt on Sinai, in either case no reason existed for renouncing and putting away the previously existing divinities of the parties to the federation. When the Athenians formed the Ionian league, the Apollo of Delos became the *only* god of the confederacy. But this did not cause the Athenians to give up the worship of Pallas Athene or of other deities venerated in Athens. They retained their independence within the confederation like every other federate state, and so did every separate community which existed in Athens or in other cities. These, also, could not do without their deities, and so kept on worshipping them as before. The same in all essentials must have been the case with Israel. The federation was made in Yahweh's name and with Yahweh; but every narrower circle within this federation continued to serve its special god as before. If new inner circles were formed, there was nothing to prevent their setting up their special cult alongside that of Yahweh. Theoretically this must have been the case with Israel in its existing state of civilisation and religion. Have we also facts to bear out this theory?

From the nature of the case these proofs are not numerous, but, though few, they are definite and convincing. The traces of a worship of household gods survived longest of all. The invaluable proof-passage for this is furnished by the story of David. When the emissaries of Saul surround David's house, his wife Michal aids his escape through the window, at night. To delay the pursuit, Michal reports him sick, and shows the officers the "Teraphim," which she had dressed up and placed in the bed.[1] The reference is without doubt to some piece of household furniture, which was ever at hand in every well-ordered family. Hosea iii. 4 shows that, even in the eighth century, the Israelites were thoroughly accustomed to it, and would not be without it. But from Genesis xxxi. 19, 30, where Rachel steals the Teraphim of her father Laban, we know that this object was the image of a god; and Ezekiel xxi. 26, where the king of Babylon consults the Teraphim, as well as Zechariah x. 2, shows that oracles were sought from it. Now it is quite inconceivable that there should ever have been, in Israel, an image of Yahweh in every house. Moreover, the tradition knows quite well that it is a question of another cult, that is to say, according to the conception of a later time, idolatry. Rachel concealed the stolen Teraphim from her father and kept it. But when Jacob comes into Canaan and

[1] 1 Sam. xix. 11-17.

draws near the place where Yahweh had appeared to him, he bids all his household put away all strange gods. These are delivered up to him and he buries them under the terebinth at Shechem.[1] The oracle-god stolen from Laban was, without doubt, among these gods, for the passage in which this event is narrated is derived from the same document (E) which in chapter xxxi. described the theft. Now it is just this document which delights to use the patriarchal history as an example to later Israel of how it should act to be acceptable to Yahweh. Abraham did not deem his only son too precious to sacrifice to Yahweh. This is the right spirit, and the spirit which every true Israelite ought to have. But Yahweh is satisfied with the spirit alone; He desires not human sacrifice. This is a lesson to the misdirected religious impulse which held the sacrifice of the first-born to be due to Yahweh. So in Jacob's story likewise, Israel is taught through its ancestor Jacob that it should have laid aside the service of every other god the moment it trod the sacred soil of Canaan. But just as we know from Ezekiel xx. 26 that the bloody sacrifice of the first-born was actually looked upon in certain circles of Israel as a rite demanded by Yahweh, and made to him a countless number of times, so Genesis xxxv.

[1] Gen. xxxv. 1-4.

does not mean that Israel in reality gave up its ancient gods when it entered Canaan from the wilderness. On the contrary, it rather contrasts the ideal represented by the patriarch Jacob with the sad reality.

It is even highly probable that the existence of the household god is recognised in the Law itself, in the Book of the Covenant.[1] In the law of slavery (Exodus xxi. 2–6), provision is made for the case in which a slave prefers remaining with his master, as his property for ever, to receiving his freedom in the seventh year of service. In this case his master must bring him to the god (to the Elohim, אל האלהים)—so the law prescribes,—place him by the door, or door-post, and bore his ear through with an awl.[2] This rite has a real significance only when the door in question is the door of the house to which the slave wishes to belong for life. And this is more plainly said in the parallel passage, Deuteronomy xv. 17: " Then thou shalt take an awl and thrust it through his ear unto the door, that he may be thy bondman for ever." Here

[1] This name, suggested by Exodus xxiv. 7, is given to the oldest legislation in the source E, contained in Ex. xxi.–xxiii.
[2] It is a remarkable fact that in one of the savage tribes in Central Brazil the boring of the cartilage of the ear is a mark of ownership, used in the ceremony of betrothal, though not connected with the door-post. See v. d. Steinen, *Unter den Naturvölkern Zentral-Brasiliens*, 1894, p. 501.

the god is completely lacking, doubtless because at the time of Deuteronomy no god besides Yahweh was any longer permitted. The old custom was retained, despite the fact that it was now stripped of its religious significance. Originally the god and the door of the house to which the slave wished to belong must have stood side by side. The object referred to as "the god" would seem to be the Teraphim itself, and it is quite possible, although by no means necessary, that in Exodus xxi. 6, "the Teraphim" once stood instead of the present "the Elohim."[1]

We will not stop over the much-disputed question as to the derivation and meaning of the word "Teraphim." But it may be set down as extremely probable that the Teraphim belong to the extensive domain of ancestor-worship, or worship of the dead, which, in many lands and continents, even in the New World, has formed the oldest verifiable foundation of religion. Besides the household god, Israel must have had cults of this nature, which embraced wider circles, the family, the clan, and the tribe, though only isolated and unconnected traces of these cults remain in the Old Testament. In 1 Samuel xx. 6, David speaks of his family's yearly sacrifice in Bethlehem. It may be assumed, indeed, that the sacrifice on that

[1] See Schwally, *Das Leben nach dem Tode*, p. 37 *ff*.

occasion was offered to Yahweh and not to a deified eponymous hero. But in ancient times the case was certainly otherwise. We find great stress laid upon the mention of the burial-places of a whole line of ancestors and heads of clans. I will name those of Rachel (Genesis xxxv.); of Joseph (Genesis l.); of Joshua (Joshua xxiv., Judges ii.). Of the so-called "minor judges" we learn scarcely anything more than their places of burial (Judges x. 2, 5; xii. 10, 12, 15). We may be sure that religious rites were performed at these graves in ancient times. Necromancy and funeral rites are also connected with this great circle of religious ideas, and the best proof that they belong to an alien worship is the fact that later they are strictly forbidden.[1] Again, circumcision, which occurs later in the priestly document (Genesis xvii.) as the token of the covenant with Yahweh, was originally no element in His especial worship. For it was common to all the peoples among whom Israel dwelt, the Egyptians not excepted. The Philistines alone, who had come from beyond the sea, are called the uncircumcised. The wide extent of this rite, embracing, with some variations, whole continents, and its original significance as the reception of the mature youth into the

---

[1] See Schwally, *Das Leben nach dem Tode*, 1892; and Frey, *Tod, Seelenglaube und Seelenkult im alten Israel*, 1898.

5

religious community of the men, are likewise best explained by referring the practice back to ancestor-worship. It was only at a late period, when Israel was living in exile among the uncircumcised Assyrians and Babylonians, that this rite could become a distinctive mark of Yahweh-worship.[1]

Quite another sphere of alien worship is opened up in the observance of New Moon and Sabbath. These, in turn, like the three agricultural feasts and the rite of circumcision, became firmly rooted elements of Yahweh-worship. The New Moon,[2] however, subsequently lost in lustre, while the Sabbath shone with ever-increasing brightness. But both observances must be of astral origin, and since there is no possibility of tracing Yahweh to this domain, here, too, we must fall back on earlier independent cults. The religion of Mesopotamia is, above all others, predominantly astral in its nature, and Babylonia and Assyria made their influence strongly felt over the whole of Western Asia as early as the third millennium before Christ. Israel, also, either as a whole or in some one of its more important parts, may have felt it.

---

[1] On circumcision, see J. Benzinger, *Hebräische Archäologie*, 1894, pp. 153 *ff.*; W. Nowack, *Lehrbuch der Hebräischen Archäologie*, i., 1894, pp. 167 *ff.*, and the literature cited in these books.

[2] *Cf.* 1 Sam. xx. 5; Amos viii. 5; Hosea ii. 13; 2 Kings iv. 23; etc.

The widespread custom of celebrating the day of the new moon is easily understood, but the Sabbath still presents a difficult problem. There can be little doubt, to be sure, that the seven-day week goes back to the number seven of the planets of antiquity, namely, Sun, Moon, Mars, Mercury, Jupiter, Venus, and Saturn, (to give their Roman names.) But no valid reasons have thus far been found for the celebration of the *seventh* day in preference to any other. It may be that the occasional specification, in Babylonia, of the seventh, fourteenth, twenty-first, and twenty-eighth days of the month, led in the long run to the giving of a certain prominence to the seventh day as such. On the other hand, the designation of certain days as *šabattu*, which were looked upon as *dies nefasti*, on which particular forms of activity were avoided, may have given occasion to the celebration of this day by complete rest, while its sinister significance gradually died away.[1]

But, at the same time, the suspicion still remains that the worship of a distinct god was connected with this day. In later times the Sabbath is dedicated to Saturn, and we actually have an ancient trace of Saturn-worship in Israel. No ingenuity of

---

[1] I am glad to find these views confirmed by Morris Jastrow in his excellent article on "The Original Character of the Hebrew Sabbath," *The American Journal of Theology*, vol. ii., No. 2, April, 1898.

interpretation or of vocalisation can explain away the two Assyrian names of Saturn, Kēwān and Sakkūt, in Amos v. 26. In the light of the facts now under consideration it becomes more probable than ever that Amos is imputing Saturn-worship to ancient Israel in the period of the desert wanderings, rather than to the Israel of his own day. A slight change in the impossible text which has been transmitted to us[1] would give the phrase incorporating these names the sense: "Did ye not bear about [that is to say, at that time, in the desert] your king Sakkūt and your star Kēwān?" That the Sabbath was made to fall on the seventh day of the week instead of on every seventh day in the course of the month through the influence of Saturn-worship, can of course not be proved, but a connection between the two things is at least very possible.

Israel might have taken up such astral elements into its cult in Canaan; for this land was saturated with Assyro-Babylonian culture. But the allusion in Amos seems to point back of Canaan into the wilderness, and we find no trace of the seven-day week and

[1] הלא נשאתם, which could easily have been corrupted after ישראל. It appears to me impossible to strike out v. 26 (Wellhausen, Nowack), because no explanation can be given for its subsequent origin and interpolation. Prof. Nathaniel Schmidt offers a restoration and explanation of this verse which differ widely from those hitherto proposed, but hardly come nearer to the mark. See *Journal of Biblical Literature*, xiii., 1894, pp. 1 ff.

Sabbath among the Phœnicians. It appears, therefore, more advisable to regard this element also of the cult as pre-Canaanite, and to trace the germs of it back to the earlier relations between the tribes of Israel and the "land of the two rivers."[1]

The practice of all, or at least the greater part, of these religious customs foreign to Yahwism must still have continued at the entrance into Canaan alongside of Yahweh-worship, but without connection with it. For the sojourn in the desert after the Exodus from Egypt cannot have sufficed to graft them into the flesh and blood of Yahwism. And, on the other hand, we have no reason to assume that this Yahweh religion itself, as the Kenites practised it, was already so complex. At any rate, we know that the household worship of the Teraphim was carried on independently beside the Yahweh-worship, and the same thing was probably true of everything traceable to ancestor-worship.

Under such conditions, it seems impossible to maintain the tradition that Yahweh through Moses made the service of his deity alone a law for Israel. And, at the same time, it is not surprising that a new cult, the Baal-worship of Canaan, should

---

[1] A complete enumeration of the traces of foreign religions existing in Israel by the side of the worship of Yahweh has not been attempted in these lectures. It was the author's aim only to establish the fact; and for this the instances cited are amply sufficient.

also have been readily taken up after the immigration, without the consciousness of an apostasy from Yahweh. Moreover, the process was facilitated by a special circumstance. The Baal of interior Canaan was not a national god, who could exercise a strict lordship and control over a wide extent of territory. The mere fact that the land, as we know from the Tell-el-Amarna letters, was politically subdivided into numerous little states would make this impossible. There was not *one* Baal, but innumerable Baals; and accordingly many passages of the Old Testament, ancient as well as later, speak of the plural Baalim.[1] Every Baal was possessor and ruler of his district so far as the territory of city or country town extended. What was expected and asked of him was fertility of the soil in this district and consequent fecundity of cattle and men. Israel could engage in such a local worship without renouncing its national worship. In fact, as we saw, such a course was inevitably attendant on the transition to a settled life and to agriculture.

This new worship doubtless brought with it its dangers. It was voluptuous and dissolute; debauchery and sexual excesses went with it hand in hand. We know from a number of references, but especially from Hosea's arraignments, that these

[1] *Cf.* Hosea ii. 15, 19, xi. 2; Jeremiah ii. 23, ix. 13; etc.

dangers did not pass Israel by untouched. But we also know, especially through the story of Noah's wine-growing and the cursing of Canaan,[1] and from that of the destruction of Sodom and Gomorrah,[2] that the healthy and austere morality of the nomad revolted against these excrescences of over-civilisation, and so gradually prepared the way for the defeat of the gods of Canaan by the God of Israel.

But even this Baal-worship was by no means without its beneficial effects. To it is probably to be ascribed the comparatively early disappearance of the more comprehensive among the special cults in Israel,—those of the clan and tribe. For since the separate districts of Canaan, whose boundaries were definitely fixed, must have been settled, as a rule, each by a single clan, the worship of the Baal, the district-god, must have gradually absorbed these clan-cults and replaced them. If then the Baal-worship was overcome, these others also perished at the same time.

Baal-worship thus became a decomposing reagent, which, when added to the fantastic mixture of cults in Israel, served to throw off what was useless and disturbing and to produce a combination much more valuable and much more capable of development. For the final absorption of Baal-worship into Yah-

[1] Genesis ix. 20–27.   [2] Genesis xviii., xix.

weh-worship brought into the latter new elements of a most essential kind. The Yahwism of olden times, that to which the Rechabites still clung, was a force hostile to civilisation. Yahweh is the destroyer, the storm-god in nature, the war-god in national life, the God to whom, after victory won, every living thing is devoted to death by the sacred ban. Where He does not exercise these exceptional functions, He is the God of the steppe, with its brief season of flowering in the springtime, and its long, desolate, and monotonous silence during the rest of the year. This religion could never have become, without change, the religion of a civilised people, still less that of humanity. Baal-worship supplied what it lacked. It brought the activity of man into continual daily connection with the deity, and subordinated everything to his influence and blessing. It established a close solidarity among worshippers subject to like conditions, and took under its protection every new advance in civilisation. The Yahweh who, according to Hosea's teaching, also bestowed corn, oil, and new wine when His people were obedient to Him, stood unquestionably and incomparably higher than the Yahweh of the Rechabites, who strictly forbade the growing of corn and wine, the possession of house or field. Thus it was divine providence that Israel in its new home had first to serve Baal for a long time, until by fresh dispensations and revelations part of this worship was merged in that of Yahweh, the rest forbidden to Israel and abolished.

It may, perhaps, be asked : What part then of the religious practice of Israel remains for original Yahwism? To this question a satisfactory, definitive, and comprehensive answer cannot, of course, be given. But we can name at least one observance whose close and exclusive connection with Yahweh-worship is attested by the tradition, and which bears on its own face all the marks of pre-Canaanite nomadic religion, in distinction from that of Canaan. I refer to the Feast of Passover. This is now, indeed, closely associated with the first of the agricultural feasts, the Feast of Unleavened Bread. But the connection is not original, as may be readily seen. The latter feast is inseparably connected with Pentecost and Tabernacles; Passover has nothing to do with these. Tradition, it is true, now gives to the Feast of Unleavened Bread an origin which connects it as well as Passover with the Exodus from Egypt; doubtless because its date of celebration came in course of time to be closely connected with that of this feast. But nevertheless the special occasion at least is different from that assigned for the Passover, and, in the oldest legislation, in J, the institution of both feasts is kept strictly apart. That of the Passover is found in Exodus xii. 21-28, that of Mazzoth ("Unleavened Cakes") in Exodus xiii. 3-10; and the provisions relating to these feasts in Exodus xxxiv. also are kept sharply distinct in verses 18 and 25 respectively. That Passover belongs to the desert, Mazzoth to the cultivated land, is still clearly recognised even in the latest narrative, the Priestly Document.

For after Israel's passage of the Jordan it proceeds (Joshua v. 10-12):

"Now when the children of Israel had encamped at Gilgal, they kept the Passover on the fourteenth day of the month at even in the steppes of Jericho. But they did eat from the produce of the land on the day after the Passover, unleavened cakes and parched corn, in the selfsame day. But the manna failed on the following day, because they ate of the produce of the land; neither did the children of Israel receive manna any more. So they lived on the fruit of the land of Canaan that year."

It is perfectly clear that Passover belongs with the manna, and therefore with the desert, while the unleavened bread belongs with the cultivated land, therefore with the new home, Canaan. The character of this nomadic feast has been retained intact in the Priestly Document (Exodus xii. 1-14), and in Judaism to this day. Passover is and is called a sacrifice, but it is a sacrifice in the oldest sense of the word. Nothing of offering, nothing of tribute, which is the conception of sacrifice as it everywhere ultimately comes to be in settled life, but a sacramental meal uniting all the worshippers with the god, through participation in the same food.

As W. Robertson Smith has described this sacramental meal from Arabian paganism,[1] so also at the Passover the victim must be consumed between evening and morning, with hide, bones, and entrails, so that the rising sun may see no vestiges of it remaining.[2] Here we have the desert, here the nomad, here the feast which, unquestionably, distinguished the invading people of Israel from the native Canaanites. The feast had to be celebrated in the spring when the flocks had cast their young and the young lambs were obtainable. This was the reason of its later connection with the Feast of Mazzoth. But precisely in this combination appears the victory of Yahweh over Baal; the Baal-feasts being now incorporated into the domain of the God of Israel.

We cannot and would not assert that the worship of Yahweh in ancient times was restricted to this single annual festival. Other solemnities must have

---

[1] *Religion of the Semites*, 2d ed., pp. 333 *ff*., and elsewhere.
[2] We may be sure that in ancient times this command was much more strictly and rudely observed in Israel also than would appear from Exodus xii. 9 *f*.

found their place beside it when opportunity offered. Above all, events of a warlike character, and, in fact, all joint undertakings of the nation must have brought with them their special rites. But we have every reason to assume that Yahweh-worship in ancient times was of an extremely simple nature. For the uniform life of the nomad and the extremely limited resources at his disposal render any wealth of form or variety in worship impossible. An Isaiah (chapter i.) still protests with indignation against any excess in ceremonial observances and large expense in the service of his God. But the simpler the original worship of Yahweh, the more easily could the most diverse elements of other religions creep in and strike root.

LECTURE III.

Priests, Prophets, Kings; the Champions of Yahweh.

YAHWEH'S struggle with His rivals, above all with the Baals of Canaan—the preceding lecture has shown that this was the import, in the sphere of religious history, of the first centuries passed by Israel in its new home. Should the Baalim be victorious, what was proper to Yahweh-worship would sooner or later give way and conform to theirs. Should Yahweh be victorious, the same fate awaited the Baalim. The victory of the people carried with it the victory of their god. If Israel succeeded in taking unbroken possession of the whole land, subjecting or blending with itself the old inhabitants, Yahweh became *ipso facto* Baal, that is, "lord," "proprietor," of the land. He deigned to dwell in the cultivated land; He supplanted the Baal; men learned to believe themselves indebted to Him, and not to the Baal, for the blessings of agriculture.

Once more, therefore, Israel's religious history

proves itself dependent on its external, political history. Great international forces, sent from God, independent of the will of individuals or of classes, are chiefly at work to form this history. But individuals and classes also played their part, gave new impulses, decided urgent questions, overcame threatening dangers. The personal forces which ranged themselves in Yahweh's service and helped on His cause to victory are specified in the title of this lecture: they are priests, prophets, and kings.

Let us recall the state of Yahweh-worship as we must picture it shortly after the entrance into Canaan. It must inevitably have varied greatly in the various districts and among the various tribes. We must presuppose a fixed form of worship—how active or intense we know not—at the ancient shrine of the ark, which was certainly from the very beginning entrusted to the care of a priestly family, as we find it in I Samuel iv.-vi. An established cult of Yahweh in Bethel seems also to be indicated by a passage of Judges, ii. 1, 5[b]. Elsewhere in Central and Northern Israel there can hardly have been any fixed places of Yahweh-worship. We should not forget that to the Joseph tribes and their nearer or remoter kindred Yahweh-worship was of very recent origin, a newly adopted religion whose mysteries were not known.

The Champions of Yahweh

Separated from one another by the struggles of the conquest, which had met such widely different degrees of success, the Israelites in many districts must greatly have relaxed in the worship of Yahweh, not only because Baal-worship was sufficient for their daily wants, but also because the sense of nationality was dying away and there was lack of a living, trustworthy tradition as to the proper form of the veneration of Yahweh. In other regions, where the conquest of the Canaanites had met better success, where Israel could proudly look upon itself as master and Yahweh as conqueror, the wish must have been felt to serve Him more zealously and to make sure of His lasting favour. They did then as best they could, and made up by good intention for the lack of tradition. We possess but a single narrative which bears witness to this stage of development; but its value is inestimable, incomparable: I mean the story of Judges xvii. and xviii. It is compiled from the two ancient sources of Judges, J and E, but this is only a further guaranty of old and reliable tradition. The slight discrepancies do not affect the substance.[1]

A landed proprietor in the hill-country of Ephraim,—a more precise definition of the place is not

---

[1] See Moore, *Judges* (International Critical Commentary), 1895; Budde, *Richter* (Kurzgefasster Hand-Commentar), 1897.

given,—a rich man, no doubt, named Micah, has set up beside his dwelling a Yahweh sanctuary. Its nucleus is a silver oracular image, an ephod, without question dedicated to Yahweh; unfortunately we do not know its form. To tend an oracle a priest is always required, an *ædituus*, or "house-companion" of the god, who, as such, understands how to ascertain and interpret his will. Micah appoints one of his sons to this office. But the sequel shows that this expedient does not wholly satisfy him, that the uncertainty of which I spoke as to the correct tradition of Yahweh-service really existed. A Levite from Bethlehem-Judah in the course of his wanderings passes by the house of Micah. He had left his home "to sojourn where he might find a place," that is to find food and shelter abroad. Micah at once offers him food, lodging, clothes, and a yearly stipend, if he will stay as priest at his sanctuary. The Levite consents, and Micah expresses his joyful conviction that Yahweh will surely bless him now, since he has secured a Levite as priest.

We stand here at the cradle of the Levitical priesthood, which later played so great a part, passing through a whole series of evolutionary stages. We confront therewith the extremely difficult question what the name "Levi," the designation "Levite," originally meant. Was Levi a tribe like the others, or was it a priesthood, the totality of those called and qualified to fill a special office? Did Moses spring from the tribe of Levi, as the tradition says, or did Levi first form itself about him, and attach itself to his person?

Our present narrative, in which the notorious homelessness of Levi is confirmed by an example, seems to speak in favour of an official title. The familiar story of Genesis xxxiv., on the other hand, where Simeon and Levi take Shechem by surprise, but afterwards are obliged to give up the captured city, seems to speak in favour of a tribe. Difficult as it is to find room for this event in the series of historical facts known to us, it is still impossible to pass it by. We must therefore regard it as a certainty that in ancient times Levi once represented a compact body, existing by the side of the tribes and independently casting a weight in the scale.

Once more, over against all the numerous and irreconcilable conjectures with which scholars have sought to get at the difficult question, the plain tradition furnishes the best and most probable solution. It is again only a question of correctly understanding the tradition. Let us consult Exodus xxxii. 26–29, and a passage of the Blessing of Moses, Deuteronomy xxxiii. 8–11.

The story of the desert wandering is full of evidences how hard it was for Moses to hold the people together for concurrent, unanimous action according to his superior insight, and to control its insubordination. It is the most probable thing in the world that actual history underlies this representation. Did not Moses stand apart from the people as a lonely figure, in fact, half-foreign, owing to his matrimonial alliance with the Kenites, unsupported by any strong and effective force obedient to his sole command?

At a critical moment—the present connection is not the original—Moses (Exodus xxxii. 26) calls round him all who would be true to Yahweh, "and there gathered themselves together unto him," so it reads literally, "all the sons of Levi." He bids them pass through the camp and cut down every insubordinate person, be it brother or friend. They do so, and slay some three thousand men. As reward they receive the priesthood and the especial blessing of Yahweh.[1]

The question has been raised whether there was no one besides the Levites who held true to Yahweh. No less striking is the fact that the Levites to a man put themselves at Moses' service, and yet receive

---

[1] This now appears only in slight indications, not in plain statement; because a late retractor has obliterated this account of the origin of the priesthood. See Dillmann on Ex. xxxii. 29, and Driver on Deut. x. 8.

the order to cut down their "brethren." It may be replied, that brethren is not to be taken literally, but means all Israelites. But this explanation is utterly impossible in the parallel passage of the Blessing of Moses, Deuteronomy xxxiii. 9, where we read of Levi: "Who said to his father and his mother, I know them not; and would not recognise his brother, nor acknowledge his own sons, but followed Thy word and keep Thy covenant." Here we have, in fact, the very moment of Levi's origin, and this is how it must be understood. At Moses' call the faithful from *all the tribes* hasten to him and lend him their arm even against their own kindred. Those thus tested and proved remained from this time on united, and formed a new tribe, "Levi." Of course the Exodus passage, where and as it now stands, means, and must be understood to mean, "All who were sprung from Levi the son of Jacob gathered themselves unto Moses." But originally the sense was, "All who are now called Levites," more exactly, the ancestors of the present tribe of Levi. But since later all the tribes of Israel were reckoned as sons of Jacob, Levi also received by anticipation his position among the rest, and "all the Levites" for Moses' time received the new sense, "all the descendants of Levi the son of Jacob." Thus arose the difficulty we have to contend with to-day. Levi is thus, as it were, the bodyguard, the pick of those faithful to Yahweh who gather about Moses, renouncing the old ties of tribe and family.¹

We can now understand why this new tribe, forming as it were the wider family of Moses, should be initiated into the mysteries of Yahweh-worship. Since it is the heir of Moses, these mysteries fall to its lot of themselves. We can further understand how this tribe, full of impetuous zeal, comparable to a Simon Peter among the apostles, should make the premature attempt, after Moses' death, to establish itself by force and cunning in the promised land, as attested in Genesis xxxiv. and the Blessing of Jacob, Genesis xlix. 5-7. Together with the tribe of Simeon, which it induced to join in the hazardous enterprise, Levi was almost annihilated, and its scanty remnants were no longer able to acquire a tribal territory. It may well be, also, that a certain aversion and animosity against the violent younger brother who had raised his hand against all now made itself doubly felt among the other tribes.

¹ The origin of the name " Levi " is a separate question. Still, among the various explanations offered, the direct derivation from the verb *lawa*, " to attach oneself to another," with the associated sense of breaking off previous connections (*cf.* especially Is. xiv. 1, lvi. 6), would agree fully with the origin of the tribe according to our views.

We know from Judges i. 3 *ff.* that the tribe of Simeon, which had likewise sunk into insignificance, was allowed to attach itself to Judah. In the ranks of this tribe Simeon took part in the conquest and received in the extreme south certain settlements which still were scarcely regarded as more than mere dependencies of Judah. It is highly probable that Levi also, Simeon's companion in misfortune, secured for itself the protection of Judah, and remains unmentioned in Judges i., simply because of the insignificance of its military strength.[1] This is fully confirmed by Judges xvii. *f.* For the Levite of this passage comes from Bethlehem-Judah, and, aside from the priestly family in charge of the Ark of the Covenant, which probably traced its descent from Moses, we know of no Levites in any other district of Israel in ancient time. Now this Levite has set out on his travels to seek his daily bread, and probably many of his brethren at that time did the same. Their number must have increased as time went on, and as they neither had any landed possessions of their own, nor could all of them exer-

---

[1] It has often been surmised that the tribe of Judah entered Canaan, not like the rest from the region east of the Jordan, but independently from the south. In this case, also, it would be easy to understand how the two tribes which had been so sadly shattered in the first attempt at invasion fell back to the south, upon Judah, because their retreat across the Jordan was cut off.

cise priestly functions in the territory of Judah, they were forced to seek abroad a livelihood in the practice of the special art they had inherited from Moses—the service of Yahweh. The proffered supply originating in the exigencies of Levi must have been met by a growing demand, and so the stream of Levites poured slowly forth from Judah over the territory of the northern tribes, especially over the hill-country of Ephraim, the true nucleus of Israel. Levites were at first rare, so that the Danites on their northward march carry off Micah's priest, a grandson of Moses,[1] together with the oracular Yahweh image, to their new home. They must have become gradually more numerous, and Micah himself may have been able to secure another. With every Levite conscious Yahweh-worship, as distinguished from and opposed to Baal-worship, must have spread farther, and the soil of Canaan been thus prepared for the sovereignty of Yahweh. Not that the Levites at once gained the exclusive possession of the Yahweh priesthood. In the person of Samuel we have an example of a priest from another tribe. But while 1 Chronicles (vi. 11-13, 18-20) transforms him into a Levite, even the relatively ancient narrative, 1 Samuel i.-iii., explains and excuses the

---

[1] Read Judges xviii. 30, the original text "Moses," not "Manasseh."

exception by the circumstance that Samuel had been consecrated to Yahweh, and had grown up among the priests of Yahweh, alongside the Ark of the Covenant. More and more must priests and priestly families which could show no Levitical pedigree have taken pains to procure one, to effect in some way their connection with the tribe of Levi. About the middle of the time of the kings the point was reached where all priests passed as Levites, and had to be Levites. For this state of things is taken for granted not only by Deuteronomy, but even earlier, by the Blessing of Moses and by Exodus xxxii. 26 *ff*.

To introduce such conditions there was need, of course, of other forces than those which the priesthood contained in itself; indeed it is very doubtful whether the priesthood alone would ever have been capable of keeping Yahweh-worship permanently alive. For the priestly office, like every institution whose activity is of an external, technical kind, is exposed to external influences, and undergoes thus a slow but continuous change. We have the proof in the adoption of the Baal festivals into the Yahweh cult, which cannot have come about without the co-operation of the priesthood. But a new class arose alongside the priesthood, in many respects opposed to it, aggressive as against its conservatism, consciously progressive as against its inertia. The designation "Moses and the Prophets," which meets us in the time of Christ as a comprehensive term for the whole Old Testament, has, quite unintentionally and unconsciously, another and much deeper meaning than that of a general title for the most important groups of its books. For side by side with Moses the prophets appear as second saviours and new founders of Israel's nationality and religion, in face of a danger scarcely less than that of the Egyptian bondage.

Almost simultaneously with Israel another people, formed like Israel by the fusion of a group of warlike, wandering tribes, had established itself in Palestine—the Philistines. They had come from far across the sea, probably from Asia Minor, had been beaten back in an attack on Egypt, and were now overpowering the coast of Palestine south of Carmel.[1] As Israel's assault on the highlands had come to a standstill, the two conquering peoples did not come for a time into hostile contact. But as soon as the Philistines had made themselves at home in the coast plain, and had sufficiently established their

---

[1] See W. Max Müller, *Asien und Europa nach Altägyptischen Denkmälern*, 1893, pp. 387 *ff.*; and H. Winckler, *Geschichte Israel's*, i., 1895, pp. 216 *ff.*

control, their expansive force, held in check on the south by the insuperable resistance of Egypt, on the north by that of Phœnicia, turned inevitably toward the hill-country, and the conflict with Israel could not be deferred. In this conflict the Canaanite cities, which extended into the very heart of Israel's territory, must unquestionably have allied themselves with the Philistines. For the valley tracts up which the Philistines marched against the hill-country of Ephraim are just those on which these cities are situated, and the decisive battles were fought north-west of Jerusalem, close to the territory controlled by the Canaanites. In 1 Samuel iv.–vi. we possess a very ancient account, which, although by no means free from legendary traits, deserves full confidence so far as the chief points are concerned. After a first defeat, the Israelites bethink themselves of the shrine at Shiloh, the Ark of Yahweh, which in ancient times had marched with them to war and ensured them the victory. The two sons of Eli, the chief priest, bring up the Ark, and accompanied by it Israel ventures a second battle. But again the Philistines are victorious, and far more decisively than before. The bearers of the Ark are slain, and the very shrine itself falls into the hands of the enemy and is borne away by them in triumph. It sounds almost as if the purpose were to depict in allegorical myth the failure of the priesthood in face of tasks too difficult, and the rise of prophetism to take its place. A new age demands new means and new men; that would be the moral.

But manifestly we have here to do with trustworthy history. For when Saul and Jonathan take up arms the Philistines are masters of the whole southern hill-country of Ephraim. North of Jerusalem a prefect of the Philistines has his seat, keeping the surrounding region under their control.[1] Moreover, in David's time we no longer find the Ark of Yahweh in Shiloh, in fact not in the possession of the House of Joseph at all, but in the very place whither it had been brought, according to 1 Samuel iv.-vii. 1, by the Philistines. For it had not remained in their land. Whithersoever it had been brought, from city to city, it had carried with it a fearful pestilence and a destructive plague of mice,[2] so that the Philistines at last perceived themselves to be no match for the sinister power of the God who worked therein, and turned it away to wander whither it would. A new cart was built, the Ark set upon it, offerings in the shape of golden tumours and field-mice laid beside the Ark, two milch-kine hitched

[1] 1 Sam. x. 5, xiii. 4.
[2] On the question whether only the former plague belongs to the original text, or whether the two plagues are to be derived from different sources, see the commentaries.

before the cart, their sucking calves left behind in the stall, and then the cart, without a driver, left to its fate. If it should take the road to the mountains of Israel, then it would be certain that the God was guiding it and no one might dare prevent. Thus the Ark had come to Beth-shemesh, and, when there also it had wrought mischief, to Kirjath-Jearim, a few hours' journey north-west of Jerusalem.

This story strikes us children of a new age as very extraordinary; but in every fibre it shows an antique conception. It matters little whether it recounts in detail the actual course of events, which is far from improbable; or whether it grew up out of the need of explaining the final result. So much at all events seems certain: that the Ark fell into the hands of the Philistines, and that the Philistines through bad experiences were compelled to let it go from their country in the narrower sense to a place which, although not wholly Israelite, yet knew the Yahweh-religion, and understood accordingly how to tend Yahweh's shrine. For Kirjath-Jearim is one of the Canaanite cities which under the lead of Gibeon contracted an alliance with Israel, doubtless because Israelite customs had long been familiar to them. Here the Ark would be safe enough for the Philistines, since the region under their control extended much farther up into the hill-country, and at the same time they need no longer be in dread of the God of Israel, since now the proper service was being rendered to Him.'

The impression produced upon Israel by these events can hardly be overestimated. The Philistines were masters in the heart of their territory, nor could anyone prevent them from continually extending their domain. From lords the Israelites had become subjects again. Their God had been conquered with them, and His ancient shrine had fallen into the hands of the enemy. Had matters ended here the blow might perhaps have been fatal to the religion of Yahweh. A national and military Divinity who can protect neither His people nor even Himself has forfeited His right to exist and is worthless. The Baals could amply provide for the wants Israel would feel as a subject people, and better than Yahweh. Doubtless there was extensive yielding to this feeling in Israel, and Yahweh-worship must thereby have suffered a severe setback.

But Yahweh had not remained in the hands of the enemy. He had fought Himself free by mighty proofs of power; He had compelled the rendering again of the worship due Him. More thoughtful minds, the more zealous and bolder worshippers

---

¹ Compare the story from 1 Kings xvii. 24 *ff.*, cited above in Lecture II.

The Champions of Yahweh

of Yahweh, could not fail to draw from this fact far-reaching conclusions. If Yahweh under the form of His Ark had been able quite alone to overcome His formidable foes, it must have been much more certainly within His power to bestow victory on the army of Israel, and thus to assert His own and His people's independence. If He had not done so, it could only be because He had not wished to; and for this there could be no other reason than His displeasure with his people Israel. He had been dissatisfied with its conduct. What had been the cause of His displeasure? What must Israel do or leave undone to regain Yahweh's favour, and with His aid throw off the Philistine yoke?

Thus the national distress served to waken Israel's conscience. The obligations covenanted at Sinai knocked again at the door of their hearts. Men asked themselves afresh what the new, unknown God required, and wearied themselves in attempts to fathom His innermost nature. And the hearth on which this spark slowly began to glow, destined ultimately to burst forth in blazing, devouring flame, was the guild of the prophets, the *nebiim*, of whom we obtain in this period the first trustworthy information.

True, we are here no better off than in the matter of the priesthood. We must derive our information and draw our conclusions from a single narrative, which, like a lightning flash, illuminates for a moment, and then gives way to darkness. The functions of prophet and king are here singularly intermingled. The hero of Israel who first freed them from the Philistines, was, as is perfectly clear, Saul, their first king. Only a much later age, hostile to the monarchy, robbed him of this honour, to confer it upon Samuel, who in 1 Samuel vii. is made to fight battles that render the monarchy practically superfluous. In fact it is represented as such in the sequel of this late narrative, chapter viii. and chapter x. 17 *ff.* In the ancient story of 1 Samuel x. 1-16, xi., things go on quite otherwise. Samuel is only a priest and seer of the old type in an Ephraimite country town, who is commissioned by Yahweh to anoint as king Saul the Benjamite, whom Yahweh had chosen to be the deliverer of His people. This commission he carries out when Saul visits him to inquire the whereabouts of his father's asses. He gives to Saul, quite unprepared for such high things, signs which are to strengthen his faith in his divine call. The third and last of these signs is that on his homeward journey, near the city in which the Philistine prefect has his residence, a band of *prophets* will meet him in complete ecstasy, harps and timbrels, pipes and zithers going before them. Then the spirit of Yahweh will come upon him, so that like them he will fall into prophetic ecstasy and become another man. When this has happened to him he must act as the spirit impels, for God will be with him. All comes to pass as was foretold, and those who know him, seeing him now in prophetic frenzy, ask in amazement: "What has happened to the son of Kish? does Saul also belong to the prophets?" Again we will not insist upon the details of the story—we do not know whether events took precisely this course—but two elements remain; first of all, the popular saying, "Is Saul also among the prophets?" and secondly, what is here related of the demeanour of the most ancient prophets, and the inferences we can draw as to their aims. That Saul was a prophet is not attested by this saying alone; the evil spirit which later torments him is but the morbid reflex of the prophetic inspiration of his heroic period. But Saul as prophet is our voucher for the actual rise of prophetism in this period of the Philistine oppression. It is questionable whether there were prophets in Israel at a still earlier time; for all passages where prophets are mentioned before, or earlier heroes are called by this title,[1] stand in compara-

[1] *Cf.* especially Abraham, Gen. xx. 7; Moses, Deut. xviii. 15; Miriam, Ex. xv. 20; Eldad and Medad, Num. xi. 26 *ff.;* Deborah, Judges iv. 4; an unnamed prophet, Judges vi. 8; Samuel, 1 Samuel iii. 20.

tively late narratives, and may arise from the transfer of later phenomena and conceptions to earlier times. In the case of Samuel, at least, this is susceptible of direct proof. For in the ancient narrative (1 Samuel ix. 11) he is not called *nabî*, "prophet," but *ro'ê*, "seer," and clearly distinguishes himself from the prophets of whom he speaks to Saul (x. 5 *f.*)[1] We can also see from the narrative that the prophetism of the time was something new, unusual, regarded with a certain distrust. For when the people express their surprise that Saul should have connected himself with them, one of them adds contemptuously, "And who is their father?" that is, no one knows to whom they belong; they are stray vagabonds without name or pedigree.

Now it has been assumed that the phenomenon had then quite newly appeared in Israel, and was accordingly of Palestinian origin, and as the Elijah story mentions also prophets of Baal, some scholars have even concluded that this phenomenon is one of those elements which the Yahweh religion adopted from the Canaanites. However, we must not build too much on the Elijah story, and if Israel did receive prophetism from Canaan, at any rate it diverted it far from its original course. In any case

---

[1] An old gloss (1 Sam. ix. 9) affirms expressly that in old times in Israel men spoke of Seers, not of Prophets.

The Champions of Yahweh 97

the possibility remains that prophetism was native to Israel,[1] perhaps only to a section of the people, it may be from pre-Palestinian times, and that in the period of the Philistine oppression it only awoke from long slumber and obtained a greater scope and significance than before.

Of the demeanour of the prophets of this period we get a sufficiently clear conception from this story, and many another narrative of even much later origin presents the same picture. More than once, prophet and madman are synonymous.[2] If we would picture them to ourselves we need only think of the dervishes of the Mohammedan world or the flagellants and similar enthusiasts in mediæval Christianity. The comparison extends farther than the outward demeanour. For just as the flagellants were the promoters of a profound movement of penitence,

---

[1] In 1 Kings xviii. 19, the four hundred prophets of the Ashera are interpolated, as is proved by the fact that in vs. 22, 25, and especially in verse 40, where they could not fail to be mentioned, there is no reference to them. If we strike out these words in verse 19, it is expressly said of the prophets of Baal that they ate at Jezebel's table, that is, belonged to her court. This makes it evident that they were prophets of the Tyrian Baal, not of the Baals of interior Canaan. But it is only from the latter that Israel in the days of Saul could have adopted prophetism. The only testimony which has been adduced in support of the latter theory, therefore, proves absolutely nothing. Moreover, in 1 Kings xviii. we should expect the priests of Baal, rather than the prophets, to appear.

[2] 2 Kings ix. 11; Jeremiah xxix. 26; Hosea ix. 7.

7

by which it was hoped the fearful judgment of the plague might be averted, and as the dervishes seek to rally the forces and determination of the Mohammedan world against the mighty strides of Christianity, and have actually turned their aspiration into accomplished fact to the extent of forming kingdoms, so the ecstasy of the prophet bands in Samuel's time was no mere symptom, no mere religious exercise which recedes into itself. The prophets also, as well as dervishes and flagellants, must have pursued a religio-national aim. We can conceive no other than the shaking off of the Philistine yoke by means of the purer and more zealous worship of Yahweh. And that which the circumstances of the time suggest is confirmed in fullest degree by the deeds of the single prominent personality within their circle, the neophyte Saul. For when the prophetic spirit seizes him for the second time his wrath compels his reluctant countrymen to hasten to Jabesh-Gilead to the help of their brethren, and he overcomes the insolent Ammonites. From this the raising of Saul to the kingship and the war with the Philistines follow as if a matter of course; no one expects anything else of him. During the critical struggle we find in him the scrupulously devout servant of Yahweh, anxiously watching that nothing be neglected which may make sure of His favour. The oft-repeated consultation of the oracle of Yahweh; the fasting of all the warriors until the victory is won; the dread of Yahweh's displeasure as the hungry people seize the cattle of the enemy and slaughter without ritual observances; the grim determination with which he ascertains through the oracle the guilt of his son Jonathan and is resolved upon his death; and, lastly, the gloomy "redemption" effected by the people, no doubt by the subtitution of another victim,—all these are cumulative proofs of the view here presented.[1]

From these evidences a conclusion may be drawn as to the spirit and aims of the prophetic movement of this period. It will be objected that Saul still, according to all that we know, did not join the prophetic bands, nor march with them raving through country and town; that on the contrary he remained at home, and in this respect differed fundamentally from the prophetic hordes. But if the prophetic movement possessed at that time any public importance at all,—and this can scarcely be doubted,—it must have made earnest endeavours to gain adherents permanently settled in the various districts, affiliated, as it were, with the order, who,

[1] See 1 Samuel xi. and xiv. 18, 36 *f.*, 41 *ff.*, 24, 33 *ff.*, 38 *ff.*, 45. For the emended text of these passages, see Budde, *The Books of Samuel* (Polychrome Bible), 1894, and Smith, *Samuel* (International Critical Commentary), 1899.

when opportunity offered, would act in its spirit. Much as we may regret, therefore, that the material at our disposal is not richer, from what we have we must conclude that the prophetic movement was aroused at this time by a deep sense of the misery and shame of the defeat of Israel and its religion, and by hatred of the dominion of the Philistines. At first only a psychic excitement, involuntary and passive, the movement became by its origin in the distress of the people impregnated with an impulse to action, which must have developed into greater and greater strength. In their ecstasy, which surely did not disclaim an element of penance, men saw a new and potent expression of the activity of Yahweh's spirit in Israel. From this grew up of itself, without the need of preaching, the hope, nay the certainty, that Yahweh would again dwell in Israel, and that the time was not far distant when this warlike God would again glorify Himself by mighty deeds against the Philistines. No one was better fitted to carry about the country such a message, such an appeal to the religion, honour, patriotism of Israel, than just these mad hordes. Be it remembered that they make their appearance on hostile territory, under the eyes of the Philistine prefect. Solon and Brutus are the classical examples of how, in antiquity, insanity, idiocy, abnormal mental conditions of every sort, were ever the best cloak under which to preach and prepare, without arousing suspicion, revolt against the ruling powers.[1]

Thus at its very beginnings a stamp is set upon the prophetism of Israel which through its whole existence it never belied. It was born of simultaneous religious and national distress; it was carried onward by religious and national enthusiasm; it ever strove after religious and national objects side by side. This was so not merely when the prophets in raving bands marched through the land, and perhaps—nothing is more likely—threw themselves as uncontrollable champions upon the Ammonites before Jabesh, on the Philistines at Michmash. It was still the case when an Amos and a Hosea, an Isaiah and a Jeremiah, stood alone, even against kings and priests. The prophets are born politicians, because the national existence of their people is inseparable from its religious condition. Only when Israel is faithful to the covenant sworn at Sinai can it prosper; that is the fundamental axiom of the prophetic preaching. But this faithfulness reveals itself differently in different ages, according to the different tasks and dangers which each brings

---

[1] The meaning of the word *nabî* is still a matter of discussion. The most probable opinion seems to be that it means the bearer of a message.

with it, and according to the progressive understanding of Yahweh's nature. In the days of Samuel and Saul it consists unquestionably in the deliverance of Israelite soil from a foreign yoke, the widest possible extension of Yahweh's dominion at the expense of Baal, and more zealous worship of Yahweh in the individual districts. It may reasonably be doubted whether the prophets had already at this time included in their programme the absolute, undivided sway of Yahweh; but the tendency in this direction was inborn, and Yahweh's complete intolerance of all other gods besides Himself is only a question of time.

How gladly would we know more of the prophets in this period of their beginnings! But they disappear without a trace, and what we hear of occasional prophets under David and Solomon awakens no great confidence. One can understand how a sceptical view of the history might wish to banish into the realm of legend this isolated appearance of prophetism, and Saul's connection with it. But its disappearance is, after all, not so inexplicable. The nature of the tradition, as we have it, is doubtless partially responsible. It is extremely meagre and defective, always one-sided. We should remember that, with the single exception of Isaiah, not one of the pre-exilic literary prophets has found a place in the historical narrative. Micah alone is subsequently mentioned in Jeremiah xxvi. 18 *f.* But there is still another consideration. When the prophet's mission is fulfilled he disappears from the scene. After the struggle against the Philistines for freedom had been opened, and directed into favourable channels, the prophetic movement retires. The excitement abates, the prophet bands break up, and the normal course of events resumes its sway. The king takes up the task and aims of the prophet, and for a considerable time does such full justice to both as to have no need of the prophet at his side.

With the monarchy we have reached the third human factor to which the religion of Yahweh owed at this time its advancement and secure establishment. No wonder that Gideon-Jerubbaal, the first who succeeded in setting up a throne in Israel, though only a tribal kingdom of brief duration, should be represented in the legend as a champion of Yahweh against Baal, as the man who forcibly destroyed a place of Baal-worship and set up in its place an altar of Yahweh (Judges vi.). It may be that something of the sort actually took place in just this way here or there; but without any doubt the story contains truth when taken as an allegory of the influence exerted by the kings of Israel on the religious development. For the kings pursued and attained in a direct course that for which the priests and prophets had paved the way, namely, the unshared rule of Yahweh. Did not their interests coincide with those of the religion of Yahweh? The national kings united in their persons the whole people of Israel, but the God of the nation as a whole had always been Yahweh alone. *One* king, *one* God, was therefore the self-evident device. When the kings sought as far as possible to unite all Israel in the war against the national foe, the Philistines, they restored Yahweh thereby to His original place, and gave Him opportunity to prove Himself anew the helper of Israel, the mighty God, unqualifiedly superior to the gods of the enemy. They fought, as 1 Samuel xxv. 28 has it, the battles of Yahweh, and reciprocally, as we have it in 2 Samuel v. 24, Yahweh went forth before them to smite the hosts of the enemies. When they thus freed the land from foreign rule, they reconquered it, as a matter of course, not for Canaan and its Baalim, but for Yahweh, who had won it thus a second time in its whole extent.

The defeat of the Philistines was at the same time fatal for the thus far independent remnants of Canaan. We have already observed that the southern

Canaanite zone probably made alliance with the Philistines and smoothed the way for them into the highlands. The statement may be made with still greater confidence of the northern, the belt of Canaanite cities which extended across the plain of the Kishon from the sea to the Jordan. For the Philistines, according to 1 Samuel xxxi. 10, hung up the bodies of Saul and his sons, which they had found on the battlefield of Mount Gilboa, at Beth-shan, the Canaanite city in the Jordan valley. And without the consent of the ancient cities of Taanach and Megiddo they could not even have chosen or reached that battlefield. As soon, therefore, as Israel had recovered from this defeat, as soon as David, after long internal struggles, could gather its forces again, judgment fell upon the Canaanite cities. With the capture of Jerusalem (2 Samuel v. 6 *ff.*) their chief bulwark was broken down; but the work was still far from complete. The fortified city of Gezer was not taken till the reign of Solomon (1 Kings ix. 15 *ff.*), when it was captured by the Pharaoh and given as a dowry to Solomon's Egyptian wife. Megiddo also was rebuilt (vs. 15), and doubtless had been first reduced by Solomon. But also the Canaanites who were living in peace and alliance with Israel lost their independence. We know from 2 Samuel xxi. that Saul undertook to bring the allied city of Gibeon into his power, and although the attempt failed, and his descendants had to expiate it with their blood, nevertheless the Gibeonites became under Solomon (and not under Joshua as Joshua ix. reports) temple-slaves at Jerusalem. They shared the fate, therefore, of all the Canaanites who had remained free and independent, and who, according to 1 Kings ix. 20 *f.*, were put to forced labour by Solomon.

With the people of Canaan sank also its gods, the Baalim. For Yahweh had now become the unconditional master of the land. He took over the inheritance of the Baals, He became the Baal, or "owner," for Israel. We have already spoken of the intermingling and confusion of religious ideas which inevitably followed upon this change of ownership. But the king must certainly have been the first to make serious application of the principle of Yahweh's lordship in the land. When in the families of Saul and David we meet with proper names containing the divine name Baal (Saul's son Ishba'al, his grandson Meribba'al,[1] David's son Be'eljada'), these can hardly signify anything else than that henceforth Yahweh, the God of Israel, had become master of the land and laid claim for Himself to the dignity of Ba'al.

[1] In these names in the Hebrew text the word *boshet*, that is, "shame," has been put in the place of *baal*, in order to avoid the pronunciation of the name of a heathen god.

The change was, of course, especially noticeable in the fate of the places of worship. What is related of Gideon (Judges vi.) took place in some form or other in various parts of the country, especially at the great sanctuaries directly under the royal influence. The honours formerly paid to Baal now fell to Yahweh; we saw the final result in the feast-legislation of our oldest authorities. It soon came to be regarded as a stain that Baal-worship should ever have been practised in these localities, and the endeavour arose to refer back their Yahweh-worship to primeval times. Sacred legends grew up in the bosom of the priesthood charged with the service in these shrines, whose precipitate now lies before us skilfully stratified in the stories of the patriarchs. All sorts of motives co-operated to form them, and found satisfaction in them: Israel's claim to the possession of the land of Canaan; Yahweh's claim to its sanctuaries; the wish to bring under the sway of Yahweh even the pre-Mosaic ancestors of Israel, ancient ancestral deities, eponym heroes, and whatever else can be included under this term. We are told, accordingly, how these ancestors of Israel were the first to offer sacrifice at the holy places of Bethel and Shechem, Hebron and Beersheba. It was Yahweh Himself, and no other, who revealed Himself to them there and promised their descendants the possession of this land. Afterwards they went down to Egypt, and the Canaanites not only kept for themselves the whole country but even took possession of the holy places. But now Israel has returned, made good its title, and restored the sanctuaries to the service of its God, who originally gave them their sanctity. It is clear that these legends of the patriarchs, however beautiful and comparatively ancient in origin, contradict the historical fact that the religion of Yahweh was not practised by Israel till the time of Moses, and was then adopted from the Kenites. The legend is of later origin than this historical remembrance. It is rooted with every fibre in the soil of Canaan, the new home.

It must of course be very doubtful whether this fragrant garland of legend which gradually entwined itself about the ancient Baal sanctuaries, was sufficient to choke the old forms of religion there, and obliterate the memory of the earlier worship. The earliest prophets, Amos and Hosea, draw a dark picture of the indiscriminate mixture of the ritual practices and religious ideas which prevailed at these sanctuaries.

Under these circumstances, one sanctuary, then still quite recent, could not fail to win an ever increasing and permanent importance—the sanctuary which David founded in Jerusalem, and which Solomon his son endowed with especial splendour. Its advantages were indeed manifold. It possessed the only object sacred to Yahweh whose origin went back to the wilderness, the Ark of Yahweh, which had but lately renewed the proofs of its power in the period of deepest decline. David set the crown upon his work of founding a new capital by bringing up this primeval sanctuary from the half-Canaanite city of Kirjath-Jearim—a city which up to that time had lain under the dominion of the Philistines—and giving it a place in the precincts of the royal palace at Jerusalem (2 Samuel vi.). The Ark belonged there, for as a military shrine it must have its place at the centre of executive power. It unquestionably conferred permanent lustre and dignity upon the sanctuary at Jerusalem. The same is true of the monarchy itself, though only down to the death of Solomon with reference to all Israel. But in addition to these advantages it must have been of decisive and ever-increasing importance that a sanctuary had arisen on a spot where no other god had ever been worshipped before Yahweh, a sanctuary which owed its origin to a revelation of Yahweh at a time still within reach in the clear light of history.

The story is told in 2 Samuel xxiv. Presumably not long after the erection of Jerusalem into a royal residence—for the narrative has suffered displacement[1]—David, contrary to Yahweh's will, took a census of the people. For Yahweh alone is lord of life and death; He will not permit the reckoning up and counting of mortals to whom He grants life. Therefore He draws His pencil heavily through this fine calculation. By means of His angel He smites the land with a terrible pestilence, to which many thousands fall victims. David repents and intercedes for his guiltless people. And in prayer his eyes are opened; he sees the angel of the pestilence just about to smite Jerusalem, when his course is stayed at Yahweh's command and he comes to a halt over the threshing-floor of Araunah the Jebusite. So the pestilence had stopped at the threshold of the royal palace and the capital, and on this spot Yahweh had visibly and effectually revealed Himself. The plot of ground upon which this revelation had taken place David bought for a Yahweh sanctuary; and where he had built an altar and offered sacrifice, Solomon his son erected the temple which afforded permanent shelter to the Ark of Yahweh.[2]

It was virgin soil. Only plough and threshing-sled had reigned over it; no worship had been insti-

[1] See Budde, *Richter und Samuel*, pp. 255 ff.
[2] This is expressly affirmed only in 1 Chron. iii. 1; but, even in the absence of such a statement, we should unhesitatingly assume the fact.

tuted there till Yahweh chose it for Himself as a place to reveal Himself and to dwell in. The legends of the patriarchs could not compete with such attestation, and the course of events contributed its share to establish ever more firmly the pre-eminence of Jerusalem, until at last this single sanctuary remained the sole survivor, and became the centre of the religious world.[1]

With the dedication of the temple-site at Jerusalem Yahweh had taken final possession of Canaan and removed His residence thither. That was the close of this stage of development; but it was not fully recognised and preached until much later, in the time of Deuteronomy.

[1] The rise of Jerusalem to the dignity of the sole sanctuary of Israel is strikingly parallel to the victory over all its competitors by which Rome became the spiritual capital of Occidental Christianity.

LECTURE IV.

The Foreign Powers and the Written Prophecy of the Northern Kingdom.

IT was the same royal power to which the worship of Yahweh was indebted for so mighty an advance, indeed for its final victory, that also dealt it the first severe blow, a blow so severe that for a time all that had been won was again brought into dispute. This blow was not dealt, however, by Jeroboam I., first King of the Northern Kingdom, whose golden calves at Dan and Bethel are branded again and again in the Books of Kings as the root of all evil. Devout Israelites might safely sacrifice to Yahweh at Bethel, where the patriarch Jacob had set up the first altar (Gen. xxviii., xxxv.). Even Saul and David carried an image of Yahweh in the army with them,—for such is the nature of the ephod (1 Sam. xiv. 3, xxiii. 6, 9, etc.),—and the ancient image of Yahweh at Dan had been brought thither by a grandson of Moses (Judges xviii.). If Jeroboam really had occasion to restrain his subjects from visiting the temple at Jerusalem by means of the worship in

Bethel and Dan, he surely must have sought to attain his end by a still more zealous and elaborate worship of Yahweh; a foreign cult would only have driven the devout Ephraimites the more surely over to Jerusalem.¹ All the denunciations of the Books of Kings are really three hundred years later in date. Not until 621, the eighteenth year of King Josiah, was it forbidden Israel to sacrifice in any other spot than at Jerusalem, and only from this date on was every image and symbol of Yahweh proscribed. On the contrary we may be sure that from the time of the division of Israel into two kingdoms, the kings of Ephraim and Judah long continued to strain every nerve to outdo one another in fidelity to Yahweh. For in fidelity to Yahweh lay the special note of the true Israel. Now that Israel was divided, each of the two rival kings must have sought above all things to prove that he was Israel's divinely appointed leader.

In reality the germs of dangerous error go back beyond the division, into the time of the united kingdom. We read in the First Book of Kings (xi. 1 *ff.*), that Solomon's heart was estranged from Yahweh by his foreign wives. True, this passage itself

¹ We may find evidence of such purpose on the part of the kings of Israel in the facts that in Amos vii. 13 Bethel is called a royal sanctuary, and according to Gen. xxviii. 22, Jacob's tithe is paid to it.

8

employs the expressions of the seventh or sixth century; but it contains good old material. It is certainly an historical fact that Solomon built places of worship near Jerusalem for the native gods of his foreign wives; for Chemosh, the god of the Moabites, for Milcom, the god of the Ammonites, and perhaps for others also.

Through the adoption of monarchy Israel had entered the circle of political powers. Small as the kingdom was, it had to be reckoned with in the surrounding countries, in Egypt as well as Syria, in Phœnicia as well as Moab and Ammon. But Israel was equally unable to live apart from these powers, and every king had to provide for friendly relations with the neighbouring kingdoms. The best means to this end were matrimonial alliances, as even the Tell-el-Amarna correspondence a half-millennium earlier proves.[1] Polygamy, which prevailed at Jerusalem as at all other Oriental courts, offered the possibility of a very extensive use of this means. But foreign princesses of birth at least equal to Solomon's could not be compelled wholly to forsake their religion. For them and their households opportunity must be afforded in Jerusalem to worship the gods of their fathers. A place was therefore granted them where

---

[1] See the edition of H. Winckler, Schrader's *Keilinschriftliche Bibliothek*, Bd. v.

their private sanctuaries might be built. We may conjecture that it would be on a foundation of home soil, as Naaman the Syrian, conversely, in 2 Kings v. 17, carries home two mule-loads of Palestinian earth that he may sacrifice upon it to Yahweh in distant Syria. We see from this that the foreign gods in such cases enjoyed the right of extra-territoriality. Their places of worship were regarded as home soil in the midst of the foreign land. Politically we may compare the position assigned to the Vatican in Rome, or to foreign embassies in every capital; religiously, the Catholic chapel assigned to Mary Queen of Scots in her castle at Edinburgh in the heart of the strictest Calvinism. Such places of worship of a foreign god did not necessarily imply any injury to the native religion. If any of Solomon's wives enjoyed the liberty of serving her native gods in Jerusalem, it was the much-vaunted daughter of the Pharaoh. Yet there surely did not exist the slightest danger that the people of Judah would thereby become infected with Egyptian idolatry. No trace of it has come down to us. The less a queen went out from the walls of the harem into public, and the stranger the divinities she worshipped appeared to Israelite eyes, the more harmless and indifferent would be such alien worship in their midst.

But if danger already existed under Solomon, the time was coming in the Northern Kingdom when these things would give rise to a mortal struggle between Yahweh and His rivals. I allude, of course, to Ahab of Israel. His marriage with Jezebel, daughter of Ethbaal, King of Tyre, arranged beyond question by his father Omri, was of far-reaching importance, in the first place, politically. For since the time when Asa, King of Judah, had summoned the Syrians of Damascus to his aid against the Northern Kingdom (1 Kings xv. 18 *ff.*), Ephraim had been struggling in desperate conflict, constantly renewed, against the superior strength of its opponent. Such was the exigency in which the ancient friendly relalations maintained with Phœnicia, even by David and Solomon, had been resumed. Amos himself (i. 9) points back to the " brotherly covenant " with Phœnicia. And Ephraim really gained in strength politically under the vigorous Omri and his politic son Ahab. They not only repelled foreign foes, but even succeeded in reconquering from Moab long-lost territory and in bringing the Moabites themselves under tribute. But the Tyrian princess had no mind to be shut up, together with her native religion, within the walls of the palace. Energetic and ambitious, like her daughter Athaliah, who later raised herself to power in Judah by deeds of violence, she seems to have aspired to a share in the administration. She succeeded also in obtaining for Baal-Melkarth, the city-god of Tyre, the right of public worship, so that his temple was erected in Samaria, the capital. Popular tradition in the story of the prophet Elijah has far worse things to tell of Ahab, who is justly held responsible for all that his consort Jezebel does. He persecuted the prophets of Yahweh, and Elijah alone was preserved by miraculous aid from his wrath. He demolished the altars of Yahweh, and only seven thousand remained out of all the nation who secretly maintained their fidelity to Yahweh. We can hardly accept all this as literal truth. Have we not right alongside it, in 1 Kings xxii., the story of how four hundred prophets of Yahweh in a body prophesy before Ahab, and in his favour? His opponent, Micaiah ben Imlah, lives in the King's neighbourhood, and is permitted to utter his unfavourable oracle, although it falls upon unwilling ears. All the royal children, the sons Ahaziah and Joram, and Athaliah the daughter, testify, in the names they bear, to Ahab's faith in Yahweh as the God of Israel,[1] and no subsequent change of name suggests that he ever turned away from Yahweh to Baal. We may therefore say with confidence that it was no public change of religion on the part

[1] In all of them His name (*Iah*, *Jo*) appears as an element.

of the King, no forcible intervention from the authorities, which gave the upper hand to Baal-worship. Even the open and zealous patronage of the Queen, the indulgence and indifference of the King, though they might win over the courtiers, could hardly gain the great mass of the people. There were deeper reasons why the worship of the Tyrian Baal became a danger so great as to threaten the worship of Yahweh in North Israel with permanent extinction. We have not here to do with an entirely strange religion like that of Pharaoh's daughter, but with the same worship which Israel for centuries had practised side by side with that of its God Yahweh. Nominally it had given up this worship but a little while before ; but its principal elements, images and symbols, sacrifices and festivals, customs and rites of all sorts, had been adopted into the worship of Yahweh. This process was still so recent that great masses in Israel, especially in the country districts, could hardly distinguish between the worship of Yahweh and that of Baal. And now this Baal was again invading the land from without, only not as a god of vassals, as the Baal of Canaan was, but as god of the proud and wealthy Phœnicians, whose superiority to Israel was apparent to everyone. Through his aid, land and people seemed to be recovering from grievous distress ; no wonder men turned to him, and forgot Yahweh more and more.

But no sooner did this danger draw near than prophetism again entered the field. Was it not a question of defending just that which prophetism had been foremost in winning, the dominion of Yahweh over Canaan? And as in Saul's time, so now again national welfare also was at stake—freedom, not, as then, from a foreign yoke, but from internal oppression. Together with Baal-worship, foreign despotic methods were creeping into North Israel, and ever wider grew the chasm between the overrefined and sensuous Court and the oppressed and impoverished people who must furnish it the means for its exuberant luxury. Palestine was a small and relatively poor country, and it must have borne hard on its people when the king undertook to emulate the rich city-kings of the Phœnicians. The protest of the prophets against these wrongs is embodied in the story of Naboth's vineyard (1 Kings xxi.). We may be sure that the case thus handed down to posterity is only one out of many. Complaint against such sins of civilisation, against the harsh contrast between the sensuality and violence of the aristocracy and the poverty and slavery of the common people is a constant theme from this time on in the repertory of the prophets. Yet it was by no means the prophets who drew the extremest conclusions from the Baal-worship and the social wrongs of their time. What we are told of a notable contemporary goes far beyond the zeal of Elijah. It is no accident that just at this time Jonadab ben Rechab, the descendant of the ancient Kenites, of whom we have heard already, should have founded a sect hostile to civilisation. The dangers of civilisation were crowding into view at just this time with such overwhelming force as seemingly to justify a pessimism which saw no salvation short of return to the purely pastoral life, in renunciation of all the comforts of civilisation.

And events themselves appeared to confirm the conclusion of this zealot; for a series of misfortunes followed in quick succession which could hardly fail to be regarded as punishments for these sins. Ahab was killed in battle; his son, Ahaziah, lost his life through accident; and the misfortune of the royal House was matched by that of the whole land and people. The Syrian wars broke out with renewed violence and demanded all the forces of the country, so that little Moab succeeded in revolting and breaking loose from Israel (2 Kings iii. 4 ff.).[1]

[1] On the Moabite war of liberation, we have the unusual advantage of possessing a contemporary monument, independent of the Biblical narrative, in the stele of Mesha, King of Moab, found at Dibān in 1868, and now in the Louvre.

The Foreign Powers

The glory of the House of Omri sank in the dust and a general judgment seemed to be breaking upon Israel. There could be no long questioning as to who had sent it. It was the same Yahweh who once, when Israel had fallen away to the service of the Baalim, had called the Philistines into the land and even delivered His own Ark into their hands. He had long shown indulgence; now destruction was setting in. Would it stop at the sinful royal House, or would it seize the whole people and sweep both together into the abyss?

Again it was prophetism which sought by energetic action to ward off the worst.[1] Joram, King of Israel, second son of Ahab, has returned wounded from the camp to the palace in Jezreel to be healed there—the third of the House of Omri whom the finger of Yahweh has touched. Hereupon a disciple of the prophet Elisha makes his appearance in the camp at Ramoth-Gilead and anoints one of the generals, Jehu ben Nimshi, king over Israel. The army assents, and without delay Jehu sets out to seize the throne. King Joram falls at the first encounter; Jezebel is hurled from a window; the royal princes are slaughtered by the cowardly authorities of Samaria; even the royal House of David is caught by the furious tempest and almost completely extir-

[1] See 2 Kings ix., x.

pated. Then follows the judgment on the Baal-worshippers in Samaria. King Jehu for this purpose takes the zealot, Jonadab ben Rechab, up into his chariot, that he may witness this proof of the new King's zeal for Yahweh. The worship of the Baal of Tyre goes down, together with the royal House, in torrents of blood. There can be no doubt that the reason why Jehu was made the candidate of the prophets for succession to the throne was that he was known as a zealot for the pure worship of Yahweh. For this reason alone we might be sure that he and his successors were unremitting in their zealous endeavour to maintain the worship of Yahweh in Israel pure and uncontaminated. This inference is fully confirmed—if we may trust the popular tales of the Second Book of Kings—by the fact that for full two generations the prophet is found firmly established alongside the king, as the bulwark of the throne.

After these two generations we come upon more trustworthy witnesses. They are the books of the literary prophets. These give us, each for his own time, an accurate reflection of the existing religious conditions and convictions. The two oldest among them, Amos and Hosea, the prophets of the decline of the Northern Kingdom, will tell us what religious consequences the overthrow of the House of Omri

The Foreign Powers 123

and its Baal-worship brought in its train. We are confronted here with a curiously two-sided representation. Surprising in the highest degree, yes, overwhelming is the grandeur of the idea of God which meets us in Amos. It is not monotheism, not the belief in *one* God excluding the existence of all others, but a belief in the unqualified superiority of Yahweh so absolute as to be practically a belief in His omnipotence. As to this, it makes no difference at all whether or not a series of passages (iv. 13 *f.*, v. 8 *f.*, ix. 6), in the nature of doxologies praising Yahweh as Creator of heaven and earth, are rejected as spurious. For the whole Book of Amos supports the same views. In vii. 4, and ix. 2, absolute power over every part of the world is attributed to Him. Chapter i. pronounces Yahweh's judgment upon all the surrounding peoples. According to ix. 7, Yahweh not only brought Israel up out of Egypt, but the Philistines from Caphtor and the Aramæans from Kir as well. He might act, so the same passage suggests, if He saw fit, toward the Cushites, inhabitants of the most distant South,[1] in the same way as He had done toward Israel. If we draw the plain inference from such statements, put forward without proof as self-evident, the gods of the heathen must

---

[1] H. Winckler (*Mitteilungen der Vorderasiatischen Gesellschaft*, 1898, 4, p. 8) wrongly supposes the Arabian Cushites to be meant.

appear as subject to Yahweh. They may for a time presumptuously imagine themselves to have independent power, but in reality they only carry out the will and commands of Yahweh. This is exactly the rôle which in Isaiah x. 5 *ff.* is assigned to them and to the kings who serve them—a mighty advance upon the view which once led Israel, after the conquest of Canaan, to pay its worship to the Baalim, or upon that which in 1 Samuel xxvi. 19 is attributed to David, namely, that in a foreign land one must also serve foreign gods! The victory over the Baal of Tyre must surely have contributed no small share to this change of view. In former times Yahweh had overthrown Egypt, Canaan, Philistia; but now in the most recent times He had also overcome the god of the rich and mighty nation of the Phœnicians: who could withstand this God!"[1]

But can we then infer that the literary prophets were in complete accord with their predecessors who had instigated and supported the revolution of Jehu? Hosea gives us the answer in the very beginning of his book: "For yet a little while and I will avenge

[1] It may be objected that Amos was, by birth at least, a Judean (see *Semitic Studies* in memory of Alexander Kohut, Berlin, 1897, p. 106 *f.*), and that these events in the Northern Kingdom would scarcely have affected him. But we must not forget that the fall of Jezebel was followed by that of Athaliah in Jerusalem (1 Kings xi.), so that all Israel was convulsed by this revolution and driven to reflect.

upon the house of Jehu the blood spilt at Jezreel, and will put an end to the kingdom of the house of Israel!" Nothing else is here meant than the atrocities connected with Jehu's accession to the throne, the streams of blood in which the House of Omri and the Tyrian Baal had gone down. What therefore the zealot Jonadab had once witnessed without so much as the quiver of an eyelid, nay with satisfaction and inward triumph, what had not prevented the prophets at that time from lending loyal support to the House of Jehu, appears now to the literary prophet so heinous, so abhorrent, that after three generations the royal House is still burdened with blood-guiltiness and in consequence must perish. How shall we explain such contradictory judgments concerning the same thing, within the limits of the same class?

We shall find the answer readily, if we recall with what hopes prophetism had hailed and favoured the revolution of Jehu. It had seen in the Syrian oppression the manifest proof that Yahweh was angry with Israel because of the spreading Baal-worship. It had hoped and confidently believed that with the removal of this Baal-worship this punishment also would depart from Israel; that Israel, returned to the loyal service of its God, would, under the lead of Yahweh, overcome all its foes. This hope had proved deceptive. We learn from the Assyrian monuments a fact of which Scripture makes no mention ; viz., that Jehu, immediately after his accession (B.C. 842), paid tribute to Shalmanezer II. of Assyria, thereby acknowledging himself his vassal.[1] In the same year Shalmanezer undertook a destructive campaign against Damascus, and penned up Hazael, its King, within his capital. Did Jehu purchase this help in advance by his tribute, or did he subsequently by this means avert from Israel the danger of an Assyrian attack? We do not know; but the latter alternative is perhaps the more probable, since Tyre and Sidon also pay tribute at the same time. In either case, the prophetic party, which had supposed all danger removed by the extirpation of Baal-worship, experienced a grievous disappointment. But still worse was to come. It was but for a few years that Shalmanezer was able to send his forces to the west, and as soon as they failed to appear Damascus recovered its strength. A period of fearful distress now came for its hereditary foe, the Northern Kingdom of Israel, of which the allusions of the Book of Kings (*cf.* 2 Kings viii. 7 *ff.*, xii. 18 *ff.*, xiii. 7) gives us an inkling. For more than a generation the kings of the House

---

[1] Schrader, *Keilinschr. Bibliothek*, i., p. 151 ; G. Smith, *Assyr. Canon*, p. 114 ; and *cf.* Kent, *History of Hebrew People*, ii. 70 *f.*

of Jehu maintained with difficulty the struggle for existence. In this matter of supreme importance, therefore, the extirpation of Baal-worship had been of no avail; the punishment had not been averted, Yahweh was as angry as ever with Israel. Why did He act thus? what further did He require, besides the exclusive service of Himself? Israel's national conscience, its conscience incarnate in the person of the prophets, was confronted with this question, on the basis of the covenant entered into with Yahweh. And again we remember that it was not Baal-worship alone which had brought about the overthrow of the House of Omri, but its deeds of violence also, of which the murder of Naboth stands as the classic example. This cancerous sore of the monarchy had not been removed by Jehu and his House. He had founded his kingdom by cunning, deceit, and deeds of atrocity; and the grievous times which followed were certainly not calculated to lighten the yoke of the people. Yahweh could not look unmoved upon such ill-treatment of His innocent people; for this reason He continued to be angry, and did not turn away the punishment.

Through such experiences and reflections prophetism came to the apprehension of a new truth. It was not enough to worship Yahweh, and Him alone; everything depended on *how* He was worshipped.

Yahweh is the God of righteousness, of morality; the supreme, the only indispensable requirement which He makes of His servants is righteousness, morality. This is openly declared by Hosea when he prophesies Yahweh's punishment of the House of Jehu in spite of its meritorious service in overthrowing Baal-worship. But in Hosea's predecessor, Amos, we also meet the same conviction. It is not for their idolatry that he threatens Damascus and Philistia, Tyre and Edom, Ammon and Moab, with fearful punishment—it is almost as if this did not even come within his field of vision as sinful. It is only by violence, cruelty, treachery, that they have incurred the penalty. It even seems indifferent whether the victim was the people of Yahweh or another. Shall Moab not be punished for dishonouring the corpse of an Edomite king (Amos ii. 1)? It is morality for its own sake that Yahweh demands, and immorality for its own sake that He punishes. Thus in principle the barriers of particularism, of merely national religion, are broken down; universalism and individual religion cannot fail in course of time to spring from this soil.

It would be a great error, of course, to suppose that all Israel, or even all the prophets, had taken this step and achieved this apprehension. We are speaking only of written prophecy, and its pathway from this time on diverges sharply and irreconcilably from that of popular prophecy. We have seen that the root of prophetism was twofold: on the one side national, on the other religious. The preponderance of one or the other of these two tendencies now leads to schism. For the one party it was sufficient to see a strong and independent nationality, and strict, exclusive practice of Yahweh-worship, the national religion; for this reason they continued to support the monarchy as faithfully as ever. They lived in confidence that Yahweh would at last allow Himself to be moved to intervention by faithful service, and would establish the existence of the nation for ever. This type of prophetism had the people on its side; its exponents were gladly heard and could count on being believed and obeyed. The other type, whose outlook into the future was not optimistic, but rather pessimistic, who laid down severe requirements and were unsparing in their denunciation of all that was opposed to these demands, met unbelief and mockery. As early as in King Ahab's time (1 Kings xxii.) we have an example of this. As Jehoshaphat of Judah is about to march with him to the Syrian war, he requests an oracle of Yahweh. The King's prophets are summoned and unanimously predict success. Finally, at the wish of Jehoshaphat, Micaiah ben Imlah, whom Ahab hates because he always predicts calamity for him, never anything good, is also brought. Reluctantly he gives utterance at last to his oracle, that Israel is destined to defeat and Ahab to death in the battle. He is not believed, and grievous imprisonment is the reward for his truthfulness.

Whatever objections may be raised to the historicity of this story, it certainly reflects with great faithfulness the respective rôle and fate of each of the two opposing prophetic parties of the immediately following eighth century; striking examples are not wanting down to the times of Jeremiah and Ezekiel. We are accustomed to designate the popular type simply as "false" prophecy; but our narrative justifies the name only when taken with a grain of salt. The four hundred prophets who predict success for Ahab really express only what they are prompted to utter by Yahweh; but Micaiah has overheard the proceedings of the heavenly council, and has thus discovered that it was Yahweh's desire to lead Ahab to his death through deceptive prophecy. Yahweh Himself authorised the "lying spirit" to enter the mouth of Ahab's prophets. Even Deuteronomy, so late as the seventh century, admits the possibility that Yahweh may try His people through deceptive prophecies (xiii. 2–5). We must, therefore, regard the so-called "false" prophets, better named the prophets of one-sided nationalism, as by no means a band of conscious liars and hypocrites, but rather as the belated representatives of an earlier stage of prophetic development. They had closed their minds against the deepening of the idea of God to an unconditionally ethical conception, and were thus no longer able to penetrate into the depths of His counsel. While propagating more and more mechanically the outward forms of old-time prophecy, they fail to perceive that they have lost their inner calling. By allowing the external forms of popular Yahweh-worship to pass as adequate, they constitute the most serious obstacle to its religious progress.

Against this stagnation and retrogression the little band of true prophets had set themselves, some of whom we come to know in the prophetic books. It must have been their very ill-success, the unbelief of the people, which above all else compelled them to resort to the pen. The great mass of the prophets had no such need: for their words were turned at once to deeds as men obeyed them. But the true prophets, who had no successes in the present to record, transmitted their oracles to posterity that there at least they might awaken a response, or at any rate receive the acknowledgment that their contents were true. In Isaiah viii. we have the clearest example. Just because Ahaz refuses to believe, Isaiah is driven to write upon a tablet in the presence of trustworthy witnesses the name of his son "Hurry-booty-hasten-spoil" as a testimony to future times, so that when the prophecy shall be fulfilled the proof may be at hand that Isaiah had predicted it. Deuteronomy (xviii. 20-22), in like manner, knows no other means of distinguishing the true prophet from the false than the fulfilment of his prediction, and Jeremiah (xxviii. 8-10) demands at least for every prophecy of good fortune the confirmation of success; only that of misfortune, he holds, has the presumption of truth in its favour.

By resorting to authorship, ethical prophecy at the same time made possible a continuous development and deepening of Israel's religion, if not in the great masses of the people, at least in the hearts of its noblest representatives. For now each succeeding prophet could tread in the footsteps of his predecessors, benefit by their knowledge, and develop and perfect what they had contributed. From now on the discourses of the literary prophets constitute the firmest basis for an understanding of the religious progress of Israel. Whereas, up to this time, simple belief in Yahweh and a fixed form of worship constituted the whole content of the national religion, henceforward one may speak of religious ideas, nay, of a definite theology, which in new individuals is constantly reshaped and developed. For the simple Yahweh-oracles of the ancient prophets, which offered a hard and fast decision *of* the moment *for* the moment, are not set down with the same brevity by the literary prophets. They are rather expanded into complete sermons; with the oracular decisions of Yahweh are connected reflections upon His nature and His purposes with regard to His people Israel, and each prophet in his own way seeks, by means of the insight and faculties bestowed upon him by Yahweh, to solve the new problems which arise.

Let us now consider the first instance of such a deepening of religious insight by reflection. As we saw in the first lecture, the old belief of Israel was that Yahweh is the God of Israel, Israel the people of Yahweh, and that this is so through a voluntary act, through a covenant executed by Yahweh with Israel. This old belief is brought by the first two literary prophets, Amos and Hosea, into connection with the new conception of the unqualified superiority, the unlimited power of Yahweh. If Yahweh has in Himself equal power over all nations, His choice in the election of Israel was unlimited; He might equally well have chosen any other people for His special possession. Why did He choose just this one? The question becomes a burning one now that men have learned to practise criticism on their own people. The more the horizon widens the more clearly is it perceived that Israel is not the greatest, mightiest, most glorious of nations; the more moral apprehension deepens the more painful becomes the realisation that Israel is by no means distinguished above other peoples by virtues of a nature to make it specially pleasing to Yahweh. Amos, therefore, stops with the simple fact of the sovereign, divine volition: "Are ye not even as the Cushites unto Me, O children of Israel?" (Amos ix. 7.) Amos does not know what led Yahweh to choose the Israelites, but he knows well what consequences follow for them from the choice: "You only have I known of all the families of the earth; therefore will I visit upon you all your iniquities" (iii. 2). Obligation is the complement of privilege; punishment, of sin. And if it is only the inscrutable, for us inexplicable, will of God to choose them, then He both can and will as freely reject and disown them if they do not perform His will. This will of Yahweh, moreover, does not consist in splendid worship of every sort, such as they enjoy and zealously offer—herein we recognise the tendency which has been continuously dominant in Israel since the time of Jehu; Yahweh required no such worship of their fathers in the wilderness; it is an abomination to Him; it is only idolatry varnished over, and is

The Foreign Powers

branded as such. Righteousness is Yahweh's demand, righteousness against which Israel in all its conduct is guilty of the most grievous trespass (v. 21–25). Therefore Yahweh will inflict upon Israel the most fearful visitation of war and exile, and Amos sings to his people the heartrending dirge:

> " Fállen to ríse no móre
> Is the vírgin of Ísrael ;
> Próstrate she líes on her soíl,
> There is nóne to upraíse her." (v. 1 *f.*)

Hosea has nothing more comforting to announce. But he goes beyond the idea of an unconditional volition of Yahweh in the election of Israel. If for Amos the final rejection of Israel is at least in theory quite possible—the genuineness of the closing section of his book (ix. 11–15, or ix. 8–15) is strongly disputed—for Hosea this is inconceivable. His own sad fate in being the husband of an unfaithful wife has deepened his insight; he recognises in it the true image of Yahweh's relation to Israel. As he himself cannot forsake his wife for all her wrongdoing, as he, even after the separation, feels himself irresistibly impelled to buy her back and take her again to himself as his wife, so Yahweh cannot bring Himself to forsake Israel in spite of all its sins. He must punish it, He must send it into exile; but even in exile Israel remains His people and He Israel's God, and the time will come when He will take it to Himself again (*cf.* i.-iii.). Here an explanation is found for Israel's election in a fact which, in truth, itself defies all explanation. It is the unreasoned sentiment of love, of personal affection, the attraction of heart for heart, grown to be an inseparable part of the life, and stronger than all rational reflection. It is the necessity felt by the man in the story of Paradise to seek the rib that Yahweh has taken from him. This is not meant to be true only of the first man, but of every man, as long as the world stands. Only *one* woman in the whole world was formed from his rib; *her* he seeks with irresistible impulse, because she alone can complete what is lacking in himself. No more than the man can leave this woman can Yahweh leave Israel, because love has driven Him to choose it. Over against the inexorable logic of Amos' conception of God's government of the world, there are uncovered before us in Hosea the depths of mysticism, a mysticism which in the course of the history of religion ever anew justifies itself, however magnificent the heights to which we soar in the abstraction and sublimation of the idea of God.

These first two mighty prophets, in whom the two poles of literary prophecy are once for all unalterably established, wrestled with the dominant power of the world and overcame it. This power, Assyria, had been irresistibly advancing, and long since had been knocking at the gates of Israel. Whoever at that day observed with dispassionate judgment the signs of the times could not fail to foresee that sooner or later this power would pitilessly crush the little nation. The religious faith of Israel, as it prevailed, let us say, among the worthier representatives of the popular type of prophetism, might toss its head and cling to the belief that Yahweh had power to protect His people. This belief was shared also by Amos and Hosea; only they saw no protection in it for their nation. On the contrary, as they were conscious of its sinfulness, they recognised in the irresistible advance of the Assyrians the will of Yahweh, now aiming at the destructive visitation of His people. It was not the tempestuous power of its practised troops, not the superior might of its gods which led Assyria from victory to victory. It was Yahweh Himself who was bringing it up as a scourge against guilty nations, chiefly against His own people Israel. Yahweh, accordingly, did not sink in the dust together with His people, like the gods of the other nations; but in the ruin of His people He proved His power and celebrated His triumph. His existence and greatness were no longer dependent on that of His people. On the other hand, He could, when it pleased Him, also raise His people again from the deepest abasement, and dash to pieces the mighty heathen kingdom. With this belief the endurance of the religion of Yahweh was ensured even after the national downfall of Israel. It no longer depended on the existence of the state or the independence of the nation, it required for its perpetuation nothing but steadfast confessors of this faith of the prophets. We shall see how Jeremiah took up and completed this conclusion of his predecessors.

Events justified only too soon the expectations of both prophets. The penalty overtook first the House of Jehu. Zachariah, the son of the mighty Jeroboam II., was slain by a rebel after a reign of six months. The laconic statement of our only authority (2 Kings xv. 10) leaves us in uncertainty whether he was the last of his race, or whether the other royal princes were slaughtered as formerly those of the House of Omri had been slain by Jehu. It is certain that with him the House of Jehu came to an end. From this time on disputes over the succession and civil wars such as are hinted at by Hosea must have consumed the vigour of the nation. Violence and immorality gained the upper hand, and in matters of religion also arbitrariness and disorder seem to have crept in. The latest kings wore the crown only on sufferance of Assyria. Menahem, the avenger of Zachariah, paid his tribute to Tiglath-Pileser III. in 738. Pekahiah, his son, was hurled from the throne by Pekah. But as Pekah was undertaking in alliance with Damascus to conquer the Southern Kingdom of Judah, and thereby to raise again the power of the Northern Kingdom, he paid the penalty of his attempt in the loss of his capital (captured by the Assyrians), his throne, and his life. His successor, Hosea, an appointee of Assyria, attempting, with the help of the Egyptians, to shake off the yoke of the great king, was himself taken prisoner and killed; Samaria, after a prolonged siege, was captured and destroyed; many of the people were deported, and the country was made an Assyrian province.

Were Hosea's prophecies of good omen for his people also fulfilled? Did Yahweh again show it mercy as the wife of His youth? If we limit ourselves to the summary account of 2 Kings (xvii. 6; xviii. 11), the question must be answered in the negative. For, according to this, Israel as such, that is, the entire ten tribes of the Northern Kingdom, was led away into captivity. Now the Ten Tribes never returned from exile, neither can it in any way be proved or made probable that in exile they held fast to Yahweh in distant lands. If we would accept the Biblical account to the letter, they must be held to have been swallowed up and lost in the sea of Asiatic peoples, without having experienced Yahweh's grace again. But we are indebted to the inscriptions of Sargon, the Assyrian conqueror, for more exact data. He carried away, according to his own statement,[1] only 27,290 of the inhabitants of Samaria, of course the most prominent and active; but even if other deportations followed later on the heels of this first, beyond question the great mass of the people must have remained in the land, and only the gaps caused by war and banishment were filled up with colonies of heathen settlers from far-distant lands.

The seat of spiritual life passed over from this population, living under Assyrian rule, to Judah. Samaria lived henceforth on the crumbs that fell from Judah's table; it had no further active part in the development of the religion of Yahweh. The popular worship of Yahweh, against which Amos and Hosea had struggled, retained the upper hand, and even later, when they subjected themselves to the law of Moses, Judah, proud of its orthodoxy, repudiated all fellowship with the Samaritans. Nevertheless the hour of divine favour came for them also. When our Saviour Jesus Christ proclaimed the Gos-

[1] Schrader, *Keilinschriftliche Bibliothek*, ii., p. 54 *f.*

pel, He tore down the barriers which separated Jew and Samaritan. The Samaritan Woman, the Good Samaritan of the parable, and the Samaritan Leper (John iv. 39 *ff.;* Luke x. 33 *ff.;* xvii. 16) are types of the poor in spirit, who willingly received His preaching; and Acts viii. 5 *ff.* is proof that many of them became believers.

LECTURE V.

The Religion of Yahweh in Judah in Conflict with the World-Power.

FOR fully two centuries after the division, the Kingdom of Judah lies as it were in eclipse. Only faint outlines remain visible, and it is not till shortly before the downfall of the Northern Kingdom that it re-enters the clear light of history. The peculiar method of our single authority, the canonical Book of Kings, is in part to blame for this meagreness of information during so long a period. Its author found little that, from his point of view, was of importance to record. But as a matter of fact the history of little Judah during this period would seem to have presented a peaceful idyll in comparison with that of the Northern Kingdom. At home it enjoyed the blessing of a long-established dynasty, sprung from the soil of Judah and deeply rooted there; abroad it was favoured with almost complete political security and quiet. For Egypt, the great kingdom on the south, roused itself from its lethargy only at infrequent intervals and for brief periods;

The Religion of Yahweh in Judah

against almost all the other powers worthy of mention the Northern Kingdom served, as it were, as a buffer, relieving Judah of the task of defence. Only by passing through the Northern Kingdom might an especially vigorous blow, like that dealt by Hazael of Syria (2 Kings xii. 18 *f.*), be occasionally felt at the gates of Jerusalem. It was only against Edom, a comparatively insignificant kingdom, that Judah tried its strength now and then, and, when all went well, succeeded in establishing its sovereignty. For this reason the existence of Ephraim and its defensive strength was an advantage for Judah, indeed, a condition really essential to its life. King Ahaz, therefore, made a great political mistake when, at the outbreak of the Syro-Ephraimite war, he called Assyria to his aid and thereby sealed the fate of the Northern Kingdom. For the first capture of Samaria, in the year 734, was inevitably followed twelve years later by the second and last; and therewith Judah's last bulwark was destroyed. It lay, from now on, an easy prey to every foe. The worldpower Assyria had become its neighbour, and every spasm in the mortally sick body of Western Asia now rent the very vitals of the little state of Judah.

So the last hundred and fifty years of Judah, which are at the same time, of course, the last years of independent Israel, are conditioned absolutely by the empire which for the time is supreme, first Assyria, then Babylonia. They witnessed the vain struggle of the little kingdom for existence. The political contest for national life is accompanied by a similar struggle in the domain of religion. The development of the Yahweh-religion is also conditioned during this whole period by Judah's relations to the world-power—only, in this case, the result is not defeat and annihilation, but victory and exaltation. In Judah also it was prophetism and not royalty which first took up this spiritual struggle. Then, for a short time, we see all three impelling forces of Israel, priesthood, prophetism, and royalty, advancing together in impetuous attack. At last prophetism is again left alone, single witness of the collapse. It towers above the event, and even in the nation's death still keeps the spark of life aglow.

Judaic prophetism in the person of Isaiah, its first champion, continues the struggle in the armour of its Ephraimite predecessors. It cannot for a moment be doubted that Isaiah was acquainted with the discourses of Amos. The single fact that Amos was a native of Tekoa in Judah must have secured for them an early and easy entrance into the Southern Kingdom. When Isaiah preaches the uselessness of all external worship (i. 11-15), when he enumerates all the tests with which Yahweh had

The Religion of Yahweh in Judah 145

fruitlessly tried Ephraim up to this time (ix. 7 *ff.*), and pitilessly announces the last decree, when he treats the expected "day of Yahweh" as a day of judgment on Israel (ii. 12, and elsewhere), he treads everywhere in the footsteps of Amos.[1] For it would be unreasonable to suppose that the same spiritual results were worked out anew by Isaiah so soon after Amos.

Another point of contact between Isaiah and Amos (and here Hosea is in accord with Amos) is that he appears, at least in the early part of his career, above all things as a denouncer of the sinful corruption of his people, and proclaims the necessity of their punishment by Yahweh.[2] Still a distinction should be noted. Yahweh's action is, in Isaiah, not so exclusively the result of His absolute and abstract righteousness. Other qualities stand more in the foreground for him—Yahweh's holiness and sublimity. This holiness, which here has a de-

---

[1] *Cf.* Am. v. 21-24; iv. 6 *ff.*; v. 18.

[2] Isaiah does not unfold such a wealth of specific observations as his northern predecessors; and when he does enter into particulars, and illustrates a point with more detail and concreteness, rhetoric is apt to gain the upper hand. I need refer only to the tirade against the finery of the high-born ladies of Jerusalem (iii. 16 *ff.*)—a passage which has of late, quite wrongly, been rejected as spurious by some of our best scholars. Other instances are to be found in ch. ii. and the beginning of ch. iii. This tendency is one of the most certain marks of Isaiah's early compositions.

cidedly moral character (vi. 5),[1] must destroy everything impure that opposes it. His majesty and sublimity must bring down to fearful humiliation all that is swollen with pride (ii. 6 *ff.*). The question *why* Yahweh chose Israel and overwhelmed it with blessings (*cf.* i. 2 *ff.*; v. 1-7) is not expressly raised and answered by Isaiah. But if it were, we should expect the answer: because the Sublime and Holy One needs a consecrated people, or community, worshipping and adoring His holiness and sublimity. Under Isaiah's leadership this view gained more and more complete supremacy as time went on, especially after Ezekiel. Now Israel has repaid this its election and all the blessings of Yahweh with ingratitude, and the punishment cannot be long delayed. How seriously Isaiah regards the guilt of his people and the threatening danger, is shown by the vision at his call (ch. vi.). He feels himself called and sent only to bring upon the people by his preaching the judgment of insensibility: "Go and say to this people, Hear on, but give no heed; continue to see, but do not understand. Make the heart of this people fat, and make its ears heavy, and close up its eyes; that it may not see with its eyes, nor hear with its ears, nor its heart come to under-

---

[1] On the old signification of "holy," "holiness," see W. Robertson Smith, *The Religion of the Semites*, i.², pp. 140 *ff.*

standing, so that it will have to be healed again." It is true that Isaiah did not write down this account of his call until some years later, after a terribly painful experience had branded into his mind the fruitlessness of his preaching. But we must not conclude that this conviction arose then for the first time, and that this principal point of his narrative was merely an afterthought. It was just to prove to his people that this experience did not come unexpected, that he wrote the account.[1] Its kernel, therefore, cannot be a fiction. And it is no wonder, after what an Amos had experienced, that Isaiah entered upon his prophetic office with pessimistic forebodings. It is only the setting of these feelings that originated at the time when they were written down.

Now the sad experience which led Isaiah to write down the statement of these forebodings lies in a province which his predecessors, Amos and Hosea, were hardly commissioned to enter. Like Elijah and his disciples, Isaiah also reached the ear of royalty with his words and was able profoundly to affect the destinies of his people. But here it was a

[1] Isaiah vi. 1–ix. 6 is a book by itself, written down by the prophet for the more intimate circle of his disciples (viii. 16 *ff.*). It is characterised by the fact that the narrative runs in the first person (vi. 1, 5, 6, 8, 11; viii. 1–3, 5, 11, 17 *f.*; to be restored in vii. 3, 13, also), a peculiarity which is not found elsewhere in Isaiah.

question not so much of preaching repentance (though Isaiah was not wont to spare the Court) as of foreign politics, of the proper attitude toward the powers, especially the dominant power, Assyria. Isaiah was guided in this, not by diplomatic talent or experience, but solely by religious conviction. He built, again, simply on Amos; on his conviction of Yahweh's omnipotence, which controls the destinies not only of Israel, but also of the other nations. Hosea had already condemned all foreign alliances on this ground.[1] And Isaiah, during his whole lifetime, gave the advice to enter into no alliances whatever with foreign countries, but to leave all to Yahweh, who could help if He would, and without whose will no self-help could avail.[2] The two occasions on which he was called upon to give this advice form the foci of his entire activity—one under King Ahaz, the other under Hezekiah. The first marks a signal failure of the prophet, the second a splendid victory. And yet it so happened that the defeat brought with it a great gain for religion, while the victory gave rise, at first at least, to a fateful error which was to hurl Judah headlong into destruction.

In the year 735, Northern Israel and Syria formed an alliance for the purpose of making a joint attack

---

[1] See v. 13 *f.* ; vii. 11 *ff.* ; viii. 9 *f.* ; xii. 2.
[2] *Cf.* also xiv. 28 ; xviii. 4 *f.*

on Judah and overthrowing the reigning house. King Ahaz knew no better expedient than to purchase the help of Assyria by submission and heavy tribute (2 Kings xvi. 7 *ff.*). Before the decisive step had been taken Isaiah confronted the king with Yahweh's command to remain quiet and enter upon no undertaking. Yahweh would find means to protect him without the need of such a sacrifice.[1] Ahaz is distrustful, and, with hypocritical excuse, rejects the miraculous sign offered by Isaiah for the fulfilment of the promise. The prophet answers with terrible threatening. Judah shall now indeed feel the horrors of war in most frightful form. It will come to such a pass that the little remnant of inhabitants will support itself, in the desolated land, by the raising of cattle, as its fathers did in times of old. Under such judgment, men will learn again to reject the evil and choose the good, and so the new generation of the future may name itself *Immanuel*, " God is with us." [2] Isaiah would seem to have experienced here not only one defeat, but two at the same time. The first was that Ahaz rebuffed him shamefully, and, in spite of his warning, became the vassal of Assyria. The other, a much more humili-

[1] Is. vii. ; see, on this whole chapter, *The New World*, Boston, December, 1895, pp. 738-742.

[2] vii. 14, 15, 17 *ff.* Verse 16 is to be stricken out. See *The New World, l. c.*

ating one, lay in the fact that Ahaz appeared to be in the right, for Isaiah's prediction of calamity was not realised. We know of no serious distresses of war which befell Judah in the following thirty years. It may very well be that the Assyrian tribute weighed heavily on Judah; that the marches of the Assyrian armies against Ephraim, Egypt, and Philistia did not pass Judah by without leaving their traces. But, on the whole, this epoch must have been an unusually favourable and prosperous one for this kingdom. For, under Hezekiah, its attitude was bold, and its power apparently not diminished,—nay, rather increased,—and it took a comparatively important place among the little states of Western Asia.

How fared the prophetic authority of Isaiah under such circumstances? It certainly must have fallen to a low ebb in the eyes of King Ahaz and his nobles. And yet the advantage remained on the side of Isaiah and the Yahweh-religion. It has been justly said that the conception of religious faith was born at the moment when Isaiah and Ahaz met. "If ye will not believe, ye shall not abide," cries Isaiah to the king (vii. 9), and in refusing the sign it is not Isaiah's patience that Ahaz exhausts, but that of Yahweh Himself (v. 13). To trust in Yahweh, to obey Him, this is the virtue of all virtues, without which no other is of value. And Isaiah, not finding it in the royal house, turns away for a long time from public life, and devotes himself to nurturing this flower of faith in a small circle of followers. "Bind up the message, seal[1] the admonition among my disciples. For so will I wait for Yahweh, who hides His face from the House of Jacob, and I will trust in Him" (viii. 16, 17). In the persons of this little band of disciples, loyal to Yahweh and to him, Isaiah was training for the nation of Judah men who stood fast through all storms. We may regard it as probable that the prophets and reformers of the seventh century issued from this circle.

We must take it for granted that Isaiah faithfully observed the command not to utter any more oracles for the unbelieving King Ahaz. He probably held aloof from all public activity until the end of this monarch's reign. We cannot say with certainty how long this lasted, for the chronology of this period is in great confusion. The last capture of Samaria, which, according to trustworthy data of the cuneiform inscriptions, took place in the year 722, falls,

---

[1] Canon Cheyne (*Sacred Books of the Old Testament*) substitutes for both imperative forms the future tense, " I will bind up, I will seal." This would improve the connection of the sentence, and at the same time remove the difficulty that the disciples are spoken of as Yahweh's instead of Isaiah's. It seems hardly possible to get this meaning from the traditional text, as B. Duhm attempts to do.

according to 2 Kings xviii. 10, in the sixth year of Hezekiah. The siege of Jerusalem by Sennacherib, which as surely occurred in 701, is put by 2 Kings xviii. 13 in Hezekiah's fourteenth year. According to the first statement, Hezekiah would have come to the throne about 727, because 722 is his sixth year; according to the second, not till 714, because 701 is his fourteenth year. I cannot bring myself to agree with the many scholars who hold the latter date to be correct. I consider the number in 2 Kings xviii. 13 to have been artificially obtained by computation from 2 Kings xx. 6. There Hezekiah is promised fifteen more years of reign after his sickness. Now this narrative stands at present directly after the history of the siege of Jerusalem, instead of before it, as it properly should according to the dates of the cuneiform inscriptions. Therefore fifteen years were subtracted from the twenty-nine years of Hezekiah's reign (2 Kings xviii. 2), and so the fourteenth year was obtained for the siege, as we read in 2 Kings xviii. 13. This conclusion does not, however, assure the correctness of the other statement, which puts the surrender of Samaria in the sixth year of Hezekiah. In general, the figures giving the coincidences between the two reigns have very little authority. Still 727 for the year of Hezekiah's accession comes nearer the truth than 714, because it is extremely improbable that Isaiah would have interrupted his public activity for two whole decades. Moreover, we possess prophecies of his from the following decade which had, almost certainly, a public character, and they are far from breathing the hostility toward the royal house which we should expect under Ahaz. We assume, therefore, that after the Syro-Ephraimite war only some seven years were left to this king.

Isaiah has set down the account of his experiences with Ahaz in the little book, chapters vi.–ix. 6.[1] It concludes with the famous Messianic passage of the prince who bears four names, "Wonderful counsellor, mighty God, father of booty, prince of peace" (ix. 1–6), the proclamation of the dawn of the better time. It still remains the best interpretation of these words, that the young Hezekiah, the son of the reigning king, is meant by them.[2] As a matter of fact, under this king Isaiah took the influential position which Ahaz had refused him. The high and cheerful estimate of royalty which meets us here, in glaring contrast to the theocratic pessimism of a Hosea, had a material influence upon the form of the Messianic hope of later times. For over twenty

---

[1] On the peculiar character of this book see above, p. 147, note.
[2] It is in no wise necessary to understand verse 6 literally of the birth of a ruler which has just taken place. The attacks upon the genuineness of this section are hardly justified.

years Isaiah succeeded in holding back the new king from all hazardous enterprises, from alliances with Egypt, Philistia, and the restless viceroy of Babylon, Merodach-Baladan. Finally, after the death of the mighty conqueror Sargon in 705, the war-party of the Court seems to have got the upper hand. Hezekiah became the ally of the Egyptians and the Philistines. From taking this step, also, the prophet made earnest efforts to dissuade him (xxx. 1-5, 15 *ff.;* xxxi. 1 *ff.*). But the moment appeared too favourable. The strength of Judah, which had been stored up so long, would seem to have demanded an opportunity to try itself. The natural consequences did not fail to follow. All Judah was overrun by the Assyrians and laid waste. A large number of its inhabitants were carried off into captivity, and Jerusalem itself was besieged by Sennacherib's army. All these misfortunes the people brought upon themselves by refusing to follow Isaiah's counsels. And even after these calamities had set in, men did not in the least repent; the moral and religious conduct of the people gave the prophet as much cause as ever for bitter rebukes (*cf.* i. 2-20; xxii. 1-14). One would expect him to feel driven to utter the severest threats of punishment, and even to prophesy the capture of Jerusalem and the downfall of Judah. But it is only against the persons of the evil-doers that his word is directed—" Surely, this guilt shall not be forgiven you till ye die " (xxii. 14) ; for the city there is ever the same prophecy of deliverance. Yahweh will protect it ; He will administer a terrible defeat to the Assyrians before its walls. It makes no difference if ever so many of the numerous prophecies in this strain which have come down to us as Isaiah's[1] are rejected as of later origin, the fact remains indisputable that Isaiah prophesied thus and not otherwise throughout that period of extreme necessity. Nor can the rose-coloured record of King Sennacherib himself, which the excavations on the Tigris have brought to light,[2] be taken to show that the promise was not fulfilled. A judgment, not from the hand of man, must really have fallen upon the Assyrian besieging army, in consequence of which Sennacherib was compelled to raise the siege. The popular account (Is. xxxvii. 36 ; 2 Kings xix. 35) speaks of a destructive pestilence,[3] and this is confirmed by Herodotus (ii. 137).

This was unquestionably the greatest triumph which Isaiah enjoyed during his whole career. The imagination can scarcely measure the depth and

---

[1] x. 12, 28 *ff*. ; xiv. 24-27, 28-32 ; xviii. ; xxix. 1-6, 7 *f*. ; xxx. 7 *ff*. ; xxxi. 4 *ff*. ; xxxvii. 27-29, 33-35.
[2] *Cf.* Schrader, *Keilinschriftliche Bibliothek*, ii., p. 95 *f*.
[3] *Cf.* for explanation 2 Sam. xxiv. 16 *f*.

strength of the impression made by this marvellous deliverance. Never had the need been greater, the foe never mightier. Yahweh had allowed all human help to exhaust itself in order to show all the more palpably that He alone could help and that He was superior to any foe. He had now overcome the world-power with the same weapon He had once used against His own people when David had the presumption to number them (2 Sam. xxiv.). And it was no chance stroke, for repeatedly and long before He had announced it through His prophet Isaiah. The prophet's reputation must have risen mightily, and the word of the hoary-headed sage must have been listened to with a respect never accorded him in youth or the prime of life. We should like to believe that Hezekiah's efforts to remove from the Temple the grossly sensual religious customs (2 Kings xviii. 4) were the results of this triumph of the prophet.[1]

Whether a relapse set in again; whether Isaiah, as an uncertain tradition has it, lived to see the evil times under Manasseh and fell a victim to them, we do not know. But we do know that the permanent

---

[1] The indisputable fact in this account is that Hezekiah took away the brazen serpent. On the other hand, he cannot have put down the worship at the high places; for this reform remained for Josiah to effect.

The Religion of Yahweh in Judah

effect of this triumph, in the province of religion, was not a favourable but a fatal one. The fact was transformed into a dogma. Jerusalem *had not* been taken because it *could not* be taken. It was not so much His people that Yahweh had protected as Himself, His city, His house. The fact that Yahweh dwelt in Jerusalem was Judah's sure protection, and would so be in the future. That being the case, the inhabitants of Jerusalem had no need to be so scrupulously intent on satisfying Yahweh's moral demands at all times. They might make themselves comfortable and go their way without care, since Yahweh kept watch for His own sake, from motives, as it were, of self-interest. This conviction meets us a century later as the most serious obstacle to the summons of Jerusalem to repentance (Jer. vii. 4 *ff.*; *cf.* ch. xxvi.). To speak of the possibility of the Temple's being destroyed became a sacrilege so great as to justify the death of Jeremiah. All that saved him from the hands of the priests and prophets (Jer. xxvi. 11, 16) was the fact that some of the authorities remembered how the prophet Micah had made the same prediction under Hezekiah (*cf.* Mic. iii. 12 with Jer. xxvi. 18) without being put to death. Why did they not cite Isaiah, who was much greater and more renowned? Simply because Isaiah had never delivered such prophecies; because he was, on the contrary, the authority to whom Jeremiah's opponents appealed. Herein lies the sure proof that the modern efforts to stamp Isaiah as a prophet of unqualified calamity, by declaring all favourable predictions in his writings to be interpolated by later editors,[1] have no sound basis.

On the contrary, we cannot acquit him of all blame for that fatal misunderstanding. Amos might doom all Israel to destruction; Micah also, coming from a little country town, might form a dispassionate judgment; but Isaiah could not help being influenced by the fact that he was born in the capital.[2] He clung to Jerusalem and the Temple and attached a value to them for their own sake. "Yahweh of hosts who dwelleth on Mount Zion" (viii. 18); "the place of the name of Yahweh of hosts, the Mount Zion" (xviii. 7); "Yahweh who has a fire on Zion and a hearth in Jerusalem" (xxxi. 9)—such are the words with which he gives utterance to his estimate of the importance of the city. We see herein the effects of all that David did for Jerusalem—of his making the newly conquered city the splendid capital of united Israel—of his sending for the ancient shrine of all Israel, the Ark of Yahweh of

---

[1] See, especially, Hackmann, *Die Zukunftserwartung des Jesaia*, 1893.

[2] There is no express statement of this fact, but all the circumstances point to it.

hosts—of his erecting an altar on a spot where no other god than Yahweh had ever before revealed himself or been worshipped.¹ For these reasons the Temple at Jerusalem had come to be for Isaiah not one of many sanctuaries possessing equal authority, such as were scattered throughout the land, not one of many places of revelation. For him it was *the* sanctuary, it was *the* dwelling of Yahweh. Was it not Isaiah's very first prophetic experience (Is. vi. 1) that he saw Yahweh in the Temple seated on an exalted throne? Thus the same prophet who with Amos declared all external worship to be worthless did much toward bringing the conception of God, which had assumed so spiritual a character, into connection again with the material. If Yahweh in times of old had dwelt on Sinai, He dwelt now in bodily presence at Jerusalem. Isaiah, to be sure, left it to others to draw the dangerous inferences from this teaching. But drawn they inevitably were, and they led finally to a practical refutation of the dogma (the inviolability of the city), in the destruction of Jerusalem and the Temple.

And yet it must be said that even this step backward had its value, and that God's providence even in it is unmistakable. For herein lies one of the most important preventive measures by which the

¹ See above, at the end of Lecture III.

dissolution of the Yahweh religion before the time of the fulfilment was averted. For the appreciation of Jerusalem remained the same even after the city had been laid in ruins. Shortly before its capture Ezekiel sees in vision how Yahweh leaves the city (Ezek. xi.). Thus only is its capture made possible—Yahweh was not at home when it was taken. Later Ezekiel sees in vision Yahweh make His re-entrance into Jerusalem (xliii. 1 *ff.*). With His return the city again becomes holy and inviolable, and will so remain for all time. Even for so idealising a spirit as Deutero-Isaiah Jerusalem is the embodiment of all good and the goal of all hopes. So Israel, for ever after, clung to its holy city and rallied round it, until for the writer of the Apocalypse of the New Covenant (Rev. xxi.) it is raised above the earth and is preserved in heaven, whence it will descend again to a new existence for all eternity.

Triumph in the deliverance of Jerusalem did not by any means lead, for the time being, to a reckless policy. Men contented themselves with the proud consciousness that Jerusalem was impregnable, but were willing to reserve the proof for the time of extremest need. The devastation of the province of Judah was in itself a disaster of great severity, and a long period of rest was needed to heal the wounds received. So Judah drew back as noiselessly as possible under the sovereignty of Assyria, and thus deprived that Power of every motive for repeating the attack with augmented strength. We do not know whether or not Hezekiah resumed the payment of tribute during the few remaining years of his reign. His son Manasseh, at any rate, is mentioned as vassal of Assyria by Esarhaddon and Assurbanipal, the two Assyrian kings who followed Sennacherib.[1] So we may safely assume that the same was the case under Sennacherib also.

The long reign of King Manasseh — fifty-five years, according to the Book of Kings—was unconditionally condemned and held up to execration by posterity. When Judah and Jerusalem went down, another half-century later, it was the popular belief that this was in expiation of the sins of Manasseh (2 Kings xxiii. 26; xxiv. 3 *f.*, 20; Jer. xv. 4). "Our fathers have eaten sour grapes, and our teeth are set on edge"—so ran the proverb (Jer. xxxi. 29 *f.*; Ezek. xviii. 2 *ff.*; *cf.* also Jer. ii. 5; Lam. v. 7). On what facts did this conviction rest? The original statement of the Book of Kings with regard to Manasseh would seem to have run simply: "He did that which was evil in the sight of Yahweh, and followed the abominations of the nations which Yahweh drove out

---

[1] Schrader, *Keilinschriftliche Bibliothek*, ii., pp. 149, 239; *cf.* 161.

before the children of Israel. He also shed so much innocent blood that he filled Jerusalem therewith from one end to the other" (2 Kings xxi. 2, 16).[1] Between these two general statements repeated supplementary insertions containing specific accusations have been made; but the more tangible and important of these are confirmed by indisputable witnesses. Jeremiah testifies to the fact that the preceding kings and nobles, priests and prophets of Judah, together with the inhabitants of Jerusalem, "served the sun and the moon and all the host of heaven" (viii. 2; *cf.* also xix. 13), and that the women of Jerusalem worshipped "the queen of heaven" (vii. 18). Even after the fall of Jerusalem the women say to Jeremiah's face, in Egypt, that they, with *their fathers, their kings, and the nobles*, had formerly served the queen of heaven in Jerusalem, and that things then went well with them (xliv. 15 *ff.*). Zephaniah also complains that his contemporaries serve "all the host of heaven" (i. 5). Ezekiel describes how men pay reverence to the sun in the inner court of the Temple, and how the women weep for Tammuz at the north gate of the Temple (viii. 16, 14). All this confirms the further statement of the Book of Kings (2 Kings xxiii. 11 *f.*) that Josiah,

---

[1] In vs. 2b the comparison with the doings of the heathen also may be a later addition.

by his reform, was the first to remove the horses which the kings of Judah had kept in the Temple in honour of the sun, and to burn the chariots of the sun; and, further, that he destroyed the altars which "the kings of Judah" had built on the roof of the Temple[1] and those which Manasseh had set up in both its courts. These were dedicated, according to xxi. 5, to the host of heaven.

All this points to a widely ramified astral worship. Only Manasseh was or could have been its introducer, and it is derived from no other land than Assyria. This is irrefutably proved by the name Tammuz, the only non-Canaanite proper name of a deity that occurs. But the other deities also are of Assyrian origin. "The queen of heaven" is the Assyrian Ishtar,[2] the sun is Shamash, the moon is Sin, the host of heaven is a collective term, perhaps purposely chosen in order to make sure that the proper homage should not be withheld from any member of the sidereal pantheon. It is, therefore, Assyro-Babylonian star-worship which invaded Judah in a strong, full stream, and swept with it court and people.

[1] The text is here uncertain. On the text of the Books of Kings see B. Stade, *Ausgewählte akademische Reden und Abhandlungen*, 1899, pp. 143 ff. (only as far as 2 Kings xxi.), and Benzinger in the *Kurzgefasster Handcommentar zum Alten Testament*.

[2] *Cf.* A. Kuenen, *Gesammelte Abhandlungen zur Biblischen Wissenschaft*, pp. 186 ff.

But this invasion of Assyrian religion is, without question, only one phase of the general flooding of Judah with the civilisation and spirit of Assyria. The whole period may be called the age of Assyrian influence. When once friendship had been made with the suzerain kingdom, it became the fashion to swim with the stream and to prove one's culture by imitating Assyrian customs. The prophet Zephaniah has preserved for us some further features of this ruling fashion, notably the wearing of foreign clothing (i. 8 *f.*). We have here to do with a phenomenon which often repeats itself in history. We Germans look back with shame to the time when men among us stooped in like manner to ape the French who had plundered and enslaved Germany. Judah had found in Manasseh its Ahab. But the Phœnician influence at the time of Ahab must have been far less powerful than the Assyrian which now invaded the Southern Kingdom.

We may well be surprised, nevertheless, that even the religion of powerful Assyria should have entered Judah along the highway of fashion. Was it not a time which had just witnessed the splendid proof of Yahweh's superiority? And men dared to introduce the worship of the sun, the moon, and all the host of heaven even into the Temple precincts! The generation immediately following certainly felt this to be a peculiarly aggravating circumstance. But Manasseh and his spiritual advisers hardly meant it to be hostile or irreverent toward Yahweh. On the contrary, from the very fact that the Temple was so used, another view of Manasseh's idolatry may be derived, which makes it appear in a light not quite so unfavourable.

By warding off the Assyrians from His city, Jerusalem, Yahweh had proved Himself superior to the gods of the Assyrians. Even in Amos we found a conception of Yahweh according to which He guides the destinies of foreign nations as well as of Israel, and Isaiah gives complete assent to this view. The King of Assyria himself is for Isaiah only an instrument in the hands of Yahweh (x. 5 *ff.*); the gods of the nations are, therefore, as it were, His vassals. Now, Yahweh had been from time immemorial the God of the storm, who holds all the forces of heaven in His grasp. He decided the Deborah battle by a storm, and the stars had to serve in His army (Judg. v. 4*f.*, 20). He bade the sun and moon stand still at Gibeon (Jos. x. 12 *f.*); according to Amos, He can make the sun set at midday (viii. 9), and has dominion over all the divisions of the universe—heaven, earth, sea, and underworld (ix. 2*f.*). When Israel later, among the nations, endeavours to make clear to them the character of Yahweh, the range of His sovereignty, it gives Him the title "the God of heaven," as in Ezra (i. 2), Nehemiah (i. 4 f. ii.; 4, 20), Jonah (i. 9).[1] Although these passages were written much later, yet what his title expresses is only the necessary deduction from that which was already alive in Israel's consciousness in the time of Isaiah. And, moreover, it is very probable that even at that time the old name "Yahweh Zebaoth," that is, Yahweh of hosts, was no longer referred to the armies of Israel, but to the host of heaven, the army of the stars. If this be the case, then in the collective term "host of heaven," under which Zephaniah, Jeremiah, Deuteronomy, and Kings comprehend the forbidden star-worship, direct subordination to Yahweh, who is the God and leader of this army, is expressly asserted.[2] It will have been for just this reason, therefore, that Manasseh granted a place in Yahweh's Temple for the worship of the sun, moon, and stars—they were Yahweh's vassals, who should have their share of honour beside Him, though on a lower plane. In this way fashion was placated; superstition,

[1] In Gen. xxiv. 7, "and of the earth" is to be supplied according to the Septuagint and to verse 3 in both texts.

[2] It is to be observed that, in the account of the official worship, no one of these star-gods is given the name which he bears among the Assyrians. The Tammuz cult (Ezek. viii. 14) forms no exception, for this was manifestly a private worship of the women, possessing no official character.

eager to make friends of the gods of Assyria, was appeased; and at the same time Israel's greatly intensified self-consciousness was flattered by subordinating the gods of the Great Empire to Yahweh in His own Temple. Men thought themselves sure also of Yahweh's favour if they thus publicly recognised His supremacy, and the long period of peace which they were permitted to enjoy appeared to confirm this opinion.[1] If we look at the matter so —and this view, though, so far as I know, presented here for the first time, can hardly be rejected [2]— the foreign cult of the time of Manasseh was still, to be sure, an unquestionable deflection; but even this did not remain wholly worthless for the progress of religion. The conviction of Yahweh's supremacy over the whole world and all its gods must have become more deeply and sharply than ever impressed upon the consciousness of the age; for a whole pantheon had been subordinated to Him.

[1] The legend of Manasseh's captivity and conversion (2 Chron. xxxiii. 10-19) proves how great a stumbling-block this long period of peace under his reign presented to later Judaism.

[2] The question how the relation of Yahweh to the Assyrian divinities was conceived of in the time of Manasseh is raised by Stade (*Geschichte des Volkes Israel*, i., p. 629). Of the three possible answers, viz., that Yahweh was thought of merely as a member of this pantheon, that He was regarded as subordinate to the gods of the Empire, and that He was believed to be suzerain over them, Stade considers the last solution the least probable.

The same amplification of the idea of God brought about by Assyro-Babylonian influences appears again in a less offensive manner in the religious literature of Israel. The narrative of the creation of the world, of the oldest families of mankind, of the mighty flood by which all mankind was destroyed save one favourite of the gods, was, in all likelihood, adopted in *this* period by Israel from the Assyrians, and incorporated in its history of the primeval age.[1] The Babylonian cosmology, which now in Genesis i. forms the opening chapter of the Holy Scriptures, thus took the place of the anthropocentric story of Paradise with the fall of man, which belongs to an earlier time.[2] But the spiritual ascendancy of the religion of Israel, as it kept continuously developing

---

[1] That the migration of myths and legends ordinarily requires a very long time does not shake my confidence in these conclusions, which I first developed in *Die biblische Urgeschichte*, 1883. For in the present case J_2, which contains these Babylonian and Assyrian elements, is preceded by only one or two centuries by an older work of the same school, J_1, which, although by no means uninfluenced by Babylonian and Assyrian ideas, outlines the primeval history without these immediate borrowings. This proves that in J_1 we are indeed dealing with that slow migration of legends which counts time by centuries or even by millenniums. In contrast with this stands J_2 with its fresh borrowing and conscious adoption of foreign material; and this enrichment of the treasures of Israelite tradition can only have taken place in the period of Assyrian influence under Manasseh.

[2] A later redaction has happily joined it again with the younger narrative.

The Religion of Yahweh in Judah

in the prophetic circles, reveals itself, throughout this process of borrowing, in the fact that all theogonic, polytheistic, and sensual features are pruned away, and Yahweh alone by His word and through His will calls all things into being. Among things created, the sun, the moon, the stars, the cosmic representatives of the world of Assyrian gods, are expressly named, a fact which accords extremely well with the view presented here about Manasseh's star-worship.[1]

It is the Judaic historical document in whose bosom this transformation took place, the document which, from the beginning, makes use of the divine name Yahweh. Thirty years ago, when the opinion still prevailed that this history came from a single hand, a distinguished investigator gave its unknown author the name of "the prophetic narrator." To this extent the name applies: that this work, springing as it does from a whole school of writers of successive generations, mirrors the progressive stages in the development of Israel's religion which God's revelation effected through the prophets. But it is surely not the work of the prophets themselves, that

[1] That the authors of J_2 unqualifiedly approved of Manasseh's course in matters of religion, I do not maintain; but they did not completely escape from the influences of their time.

is, of such prophets as are represented in the canonical prophetic books. The school of Isaiah, which under Ahaz had withdrawn in sharpest disapproval from public life, can hardly have so far adopted the Assyrian fashion. It must rather have followed all the signs of the times with pain and dread, and have waited for better times as once its master Isaiah had done.

The introduction of such radical innovations must also have failed to find general and unconditional approval among the priests of the Temple. It can hardly have been accomplished without a struggle, and the minority probably submitted only with an uneasy conscience. This conscientious minority may even have had support from without. At the downfall of the Northern Kingdom, Judah became its spiritual heir. The Ephraimite historical work, which included the oldest law-book (the "Covenant Book," mentioned above, Ex. xxi.–xxiii.), and the writings of the prophets of the North then made their way into the South. We must conceive of them as carried thither and guarded by the most zealous representatives of a pure Yahweh-worship, who preferred exile to life under a foreign sovereignty in fellowship with the heathen. Warned by the terrible fate of their native land, these same immigrants, among whom were doubtless many of the priestly rank, must have followed with horror the course of affairs under

Manasseh. Such men could not fail to see that Judah was taking the same course which had led Ephraim to destruction. They must, therefore, have swelled the silent opposition and quickened the conscience of the minority to the extent of their ability. Idolatry remained idolatry under whatever mask, and the fall of the Northern Kingdom showed that Yahweh was not disposed to tolerate it.

All these silently accumulated forces united for a bold and earnest attack on the prevailing system of syncretism. The contest was for the rescue of the religion of Israel, and the preservation of Judah from the threatening judgement. It was seen that the preaching of the prophets alone would not suffice. For the effect of their preaching was dependent on the uncertain possibility of finding receptive hearts, and opposing currents were setting all too narrow limits to its success. What was needed was active interference, an unsparing sweeping away of the abuses, an emphatic inculcation of right conduct, especially in the rising generation. These demands were formulated in a book in which law and sermon are quite peculiarly combined, so that we constantly hear together the voices of priest and prophet. I refer to Deuteronomy.

It is one of the most absolutely assured results of Biblical criticism that Deuteronomy arose at this period, either toward the close of Manasseh's reign or, what is more probable, at the beginning of the reign of his grandson Josiah, after the short reign of his son Amon. No objection of any sort, no attempts at harmonising, can shake the conclusion that this work can be understood *only* as the product of the period of foreign influence under Manasseh, as the program of the strict Yahwistic party after it had lived through just these experiences. Its claim to be the law-book of Moses is meant in all seriousness and is objectively justified. For it had adopted all that had appeared up to that time with claim to Mosaic authority. This was, in the first place, the civil code of the Ephraimite North in the reconstructed and expanded form which it received in the South (Ex. xx.–xxiii.).[1] From this was rejected only that which seemed ill-fitted to a popular book, because of its special juristic and formal character.[2] The Judaic collections of old judicial decisions to which Mosaic authority was attributed were also added to the rest, so that Deuteronomy, without doubt, constituted the most complete collection of laws which had ever existed in Israel.

[1] The older ceremonial Decalogue of J is worked in at the close, in chap. xxiii. (*cf.* Ex. xxxiv.) ; the later moral Decalogue of E is prefixed, in chap. xx.

[2] Steuernagel's opposing contention (*Handkommentar zum Alten Testament*, i. 3, 1, p. xxvi. *f.*) cannot be regarded as overthrowing this view.

But the leading and all-controlling thought certainly had its origin in the sad experiences of the present. This thought was: pure Yahweh-worship at any price, without image or symbol, and, above all, free from all intermixture with foreign cults. There prevails in Deuteronomy an unbounded abhorrence, a nameless dread, of all that can be called foreign. Every alien contact must be avoided in order that no infection with the germs of religious disease may be possible. Judah must be completely isolated, every possibility of being influenced by foreign cults must be removed. The speaker is Moses, and therefore the dangers must necessarily be stated in the forms of his time. When Israel enters the promised land it must destroy all the peoples of Canaan, root and branch, in order that they may not infect Israel with their idolatry (vii. 1 *ff.*). This is preached again and again. But in the most important passages the gaze sweeps also into the distance. Everyone shall be pitilessly destroyed who tries to lead the people away to the worship of other gods, to gods *whom Israel had thus far not known, the gods of the nations near and far, from one end of the earth to the other* (xiii. 3, 8, 14). The Assyrians are here referred to, though not named. And where the "other gods" are more definitely specified, they are "the sun or the moon or all the host of heaven"

(xvii. 3), just the gods, that is, who became dangerous to Israel in the seventh century and not before. Quite in line therewith is the assertion of the somewhat later introduction (iv. 19) with regard to the stars, namely, that Yahweh had appointed them over all the nations under the whole heaven. What reason, then, has Israel for showing honour to these His creatures?

True, there is another factor in the fundamental provisions of Deuteronomy, which seems indeed to occupy the foreground. The principle of the inviolability of the Temple at Jerusalem, for which Isaiah had prepared the way and which the deliverance of Jerusalem had confirmed, is here carried to its ultimate logical consequences. If the Temple is the only earthly dwelling of Yahweh, then it is only there that He is to be found. Therefore He can be worshipped only there. For *this* reason every cult of Yahweh outside of Jerusalem is strictly forbidden. For *this* reason the celebration of the primitive feasts is transferred to Jerusalem, so that they are completely divested of their ancient character, which bound them to the district and the family. For *this* reason the slaughter of beasts of flock or herd as such, which up to that time had always had a sacrificial character, is stripped of its old sacred nature and degraded to a purely indifferent and secular act (chap. xii.). How much of old and deeply rooted religious practice was here swept away at a stroke! But all this counted for nothing with men who were conscious of doing Yahweh's will in thus centralising all worship in the capital, and thereby averting His otherwise unavoidable wrath. How much misfortune might have been avoided, these men thought, if Yahweh's purpose in revealing Himself at the Temple site had been correctly interpreted from the beginning on, and no other cult had ever been tolerated by Solomon or his successors![1] But this centralisation appeared, besides, to be the only effectual means for preventing all infection by heathen cults. For here, at the single, central sanctuary, not only could one be sure of finding complete comprehension of the nature of Yahweh-worship, but it was possible, at the same time, to exercise so careful a supervision that no abuse could creep in. There was danger, first, from those elements of the old Baal cult which had not been wholly absorbed by the Yahweh-worship, and consequently had been condemned by the pure religious views of the prophets—sacred stones and sacred posts and what-

[1] This idea forms the leading motive of the Books of Kings, the frame in which the Deuteronomistic redaction has set the history of each reign. Every king from Solomon on is tried by this criterion: Did he recognise the exclusive right of the Temple in Jerusalem or not? and only Hezekiah and Josiah receive unqualified approval.

ever else there may have been (xvi. 21 *f.*). But it was no less important to guard against the whole Assyrian cult of secondary deities and intermediate beings which had invaded the land and by which, in recent times, such disastrous confusion had been introduced into the religious praxis of Israel.

It may appear strange enough that the monopoly of the Yahweh-worship should have been given to the very temple at which these abuses had found so hospitable a home, and, for the most part, probably the only home in all Judah. But this was to be radically changed. The members of the priesthood who co-operated in composing Deuteronomy were conscious of their own pure purpose. If they won the victory, they would be able, and were determined, to remove all opposition, so that the same sanctuary which had been up to this time the seat of all abuses should keep itself in the future spotlessly pure. But for this there was need of a third member of the alliance, the king. The Temple had been from the first a royal sanctuary, belonging to the royal palace. Its first priest, Zadok, had been a priest in the royal service before the Temple was built (2 Sam. viii. 17 ; xv. 24 *ff.*). So the house, its personnel, and all that was transacted within its precincts stood under the supervision of the king and depended on his will. Therefore no intentions, however good, could accomplish anything if unsupported by the executive power vested in the king. Such support was not to be thought of under Manasseh, nor, as it would seem, under Amon. Josiah was a child of eight years when he mounted the throne, and those who held the reins of government during his minority could hardly give assurance of the needful apprehension, much less the indispensable unity, firmness, and enthusiasm. It was not till Josiah had grown into full independence, obviously under peculiarly favourable auspices, that the attack was risked and a complete victory won.

In the eighteenth year of Josiah, Hilkiah the chief priest delivered the "book of the law," that is, the nucleus of Deuteronomy,[1] into the hands of the royal secretary Shaphan, who brought it to the King and read it before him (2 Kings xxii. 3 *ff.*). The statement of Hilkiah that he found the book in the Temple has given rise to much discussion, and no little offence has been taken at the date assigned the book by critical research. We have no means of determining whether, or in what degree, this statement departed from the simple truth. But we can say with confidence that it was not by virtue of the

---

[1] For the analysis which separates the original book from the subsequent amplifications and recasting to which it has been subjected, the reader is referred to works on Old Testament Introduction.

credence given to this statement of Hilkiah's that the book produced such a deep impression and such mighty results. It was because its contents took hold on men's consciences and they recognised in its ordinances the only thing that could be of help to Judah. And the guarantee of divine authority for the book was not sought by careful investigation regarding the circumstances of its discovery, nor by testing the age of the manuscript; it was sought through a Yahweh-oracle procured by the King's command from the prophetess Huldah (verse 12 *ff.*). We also may, in like manner, rest content with the *testimonium spiritus sancti internum*.

At any rate, the result was a burning enthusiasm, an overflow of zeal and believing obedience, which must awaken our admiration. All the forces of the kingdom placed themselves at the young King's disposal and swore with him to carry out the requirements of the "book of the law." The Temple was thoroughly purified. Jerusalem and its environs were purged of all that was heathen. The places of worship throughout the land were closed and desecrated; their priests, for greater security against violations of the law, were brought up to Jerusalem and confined there. At the Feast of the Passover, for the first time in the history of Israel, the whole nation was bidden to a common simultaneous feast in Jerusalem. It was a time of first love, of goodwill, of a pure conscience. The reform had not been won at the cost of unheard-of deeds of blood, as Jehu's had been; the more, therefore, could all participants rejoice in the result. To be sure, not everybody can have been in accord with what had been done. But opposition probably remained silent in the face of such great successes; and where illegal religious practices still existed from conscientious or superstitious motives, they appear to have been carried on wholly in secret. Thus joy and thanksgiving would seem to have prevailed, especially in Jerusalem itself, and therewith the firm conviction that Judah was now saved, that Yahweh would now show it His full favour and would fight for it in all dangers.

The events of the time appeared to confirm this belief. The power of the Assyrian kingdom must have declined rapidly in this period, and in proportion as it declined the vassal state of Judah could breathe more freely and accustom itself anew to the consciousness of standing under no other sovereignty than that of Yahweh, its God.[1] But men had reckoned without their host. The other powers of Western Asia now got ready to enter into the rich

[1] The prophet Habakkuk expects from the Chaldeans, at the same time with the overthrow of the Assyrian kingdom, the liberation of Western Asia and especially Judah (read Hab. i. and ii. in the following order of verses: i. 2-4, 12-17; ii. 1-4; i. 6-11; ii. 5 *ff.*).

heritage of Assyria; Egypt also was unwilling to renounce its claim, and Palestine above all, Egypt's old possession in the second millennium before Christ, was a part of its share. Pharaoh Necho accordingly set out to occupy Palestine and Syria. With the first step over Judah's frontier he had profaned the inalienable possession of Yahweh. Josiah with his little company went out to meet him in the consciousness of his duty to protect this possession, and in firm faith that Yahweh would go before him into battle and annihilate the Egyptians. He paid the price of this faith with his life in the battle at Megiddo (2 Kings xxiii. 29 *f.*)—or was it some Migdol in Judah?[1]—and the first result was simply that Judah exchanged the sovereignty of Assyria for that of Egypt. But a sadder consequence by far was the sinking into the grave with Josiah of the glad faith that Israel was living in the favour of Yahweh, and was thereby safe from all misfortune. Josiah was succeeded by Jehoiakim, a despot without character. Faith and religious devotion were succeeded by cynical scepticism and an unscrupulous diplomatic seesaw, which thought to make up for failing resources by shrewd calculation. Judah was ripe for destruction less than twenty years after it touched the highest point of its development.

[1] Herodotus has Μάγδωλος.

LECTURE VI.

The Collapse of Judah, and the Bases of its Re-establishment.

IT is not the task of these lectures to give in detail the drama of the fall of Judah and Jerusalem. We are dealing with the religious history of Israel and not with its political history. It was politically the same old story of trust in the neighbouring Egypt and depreciation of the far-off Babylonia and its new rulers, the Chaldeans. Josiah's son Jehoahaz, who was his first successor, was not acknowledged by Necho, but made a prisoner and sent away to Egypt (2 Kings xxiii. 31–34). His brother Jehoiakim became king by the grace of Necho. In the year 605 B.C., Necho was defeated at Carchemish on the Euphrates, and Western Asia came into the possession of the young kingdom of the Chaldeans. But King Jehoiakim hesitated as long as he could to exchange the Egyptian vassalage for the Chaldean. And only three years after the change had been made he rebelled, and thus brought upon the land the vengeance of Nebuchadnezzar. The King himself died during the first agitations of war, and after a siege of three months his young son Jehoiachin had to surrender Jerusalem and go into captivity with many of his nobles and warriors (597 B.C.). His uncle Mattaniah, another son of Josiah, was placed upon the throne, as Babylonian vassal, his name being changed to Zedekiah. The same tragedy was again enacted, but now for the last time. A first attempt at rebellion in Zedekiah's fourth year ended in his submission (Jer. li. 59-64). In the ninth year the temptation proved too strong, and Judah turned again to its deceptive friend Egypt. Nebuchadnezzar appeared immediately and laid siege to Jerusalem. The city fell in July, 586, after a siege of eighteen months. State and royalty came to an end; city and temple were pitilessly destroyed; nationality and worship were no more. The leading personages, as many as still survived, were carried away into captivity in Babylon.

What, now, were the guiding religious ideas of this last period of independence? Or did men go to their doom without religion and without thinking of God? We cannot assume this. In fact the express proof that it was not so lies in that firmly rooted conviction of the people of which we have already spoken. Men were conscious of suffering for the sins of their fathers (the people of Manasseh's time), and not for their own sins. They believed, therefore, that they had remained true to the obligations which they had assumed at Josiah's reform. And so they had, if we look at it from their point of view. Deuteronomy remained the law-book in force in the community, and the public worship at the Temple was still conducted according to its prescriptions. The open profanation of the Temple was doubtless no longer tolerated. It is more questionable whether the worship at the high places round about in the land was so completely stamped out under Jehoiakim and Zedekiah as the reform of Josiah prescribed. When the first zeal had abated, and especially after the sudden death of Josiah, doubts may have arisen in the minds of men as to whether they had really done Yahweh's pleasure in smothering His sacrificial fires and destroying His altars throughout the length and breadth of the land. We cannot help thinking of the noteworthy parallel at the time of the capture of Babylon by the Persians (538). The Chaldean king had the images of the gods brought up to Babylon from many cities, probably as a last resort for the protection of the capital. But the city fell, and men saw in its fall the proof that the gods were angry at this action—the first thing which the conqueror Cyrus had to do was to send every god back to his city.¹ And so in Judah, under Jehoiakim, many a priest of the high places may have returned from Jerusalem to his native town, there to resume, more or less secretly, with more or less general approval of his fellow-citizens, the worship of Yahweh at the old district shrine. At least the discourses of the prophets who lived through these times ring with complaints of the worship at the high places.²

But it appears that serious trespasses against the cult were not lacking even in Jerusalem and at the Temple. As is generally the case, the worse matters became, the nearer ruin approached, the more all sorts of old superstitions grew up luxuriantly beside the *opus operatum* of a zealous and legitimate worship. We find Jeremiah's censure of the sacrificial cult (vii. 21 *ff.*) standing between denunciations of the worship of "the queen of heaven" (vii. 16 *ff.*) on the one side and the abominable child-sacrifice on the other (vii. 29 *ff.*). And Ezekiel saw at the Temple men worshipping the sun and women weeping for Tammuz (viii. 14 *ff.*).

If this was the case with the external cult, men must have paid still less heed to the specifically

---
¹ *Cf.* Cyrus cylinder, l. 30 *ff.*; Nabunaid-Cyrus chronicle, Rev. l. 9 *ff.*, 21 *f.* (Schrader, *Keilinschriftliche Bibliothek*, iii., 2, pp. 127, 133, 135).
² See, among many passages, Jer. xiii. 27, xvii. 2; Ezek. vi. 13.

prophetic demands for purity of life and consideration for one's neighbour. The court of a tyrant like Jehoiakim was without doubt just as good soil as that of the Northern Kingdom for vices and errors of every sort; and even though Zedekiah appears to have been personally less to blame, his courtiers, against whom he was so often powerless, probably took good care that the conditions did not improve. Taking it all in all, hardly more than the semblance of a lawful procedure remained. Still this outward semblance sufficed completely, as we have seen, to quiet the conscience of the people. The old dogma of the inviolability of Jerusalem, supported by the consciousness of ritual propriety, asserted itself all the more proudly. Men felt themselves perfectly safe for the final crisis in the protection of the Temple in which Yahweh Himself dwelt. They did all they could, to be sure, for the safety and welfare of the state of Judah by making a shrewd use of the political conditions. But they did not for a moment doubt that, if matters came to the worst, Yahweh would interpose with might, as He had done a century before, and destroy the besiegers beneath the walls of Jerusalem. Even the bitter experience of the year 597 was hardly able to shake this belief for any length of time. For the young and inexperienced King, Jehoiachin, who surrendered the city at that time, had lacked perfect faith. It was a just punishment that he and his counsellors had to go into exile. The true Israel, however, had been allowed to remain in Yahweh's presence. It felt itself, therefore, all the safer in the conviction of its own righteousness as compared with the guilt of those who had been branded by Yahweh's sentence. If the danger of capture should again arise, they would not lose hope as the others had done, but would trust in Yahweh's help, which *had* to come sooner or later.[1]

This picture of the average religious position of the people is by no means a product of the imagination, nor based on simple conjecture. Every trait is assured and guaranteed by the indisputable testimony of the faithful prophet who lived through this whole time, in the very midst of its critical events, and contemplated them from a superior height; I mean, of course, the prophet Jeremiah. Jeremiah was born of priestly stock in the little town of Anathoth, not far from Jerusalem, and was probably a descendant of Abiathar, the priest of David (2 Kings ii. 26). He was called to prophetic office in the thirteenth year of King Josiah. We know very

---

[1] The attitude of the Zealots before the capture of Jerusalem in 70 A.D. was exactly the same.

little of the first five years of his activity, that is, the five years preceding Josiah's reform, and hardly any more of his relation to this latter event. It was Huldah, a prophetess otherwise unknown to us, and not Jeremiah, who was consulted in Josiah's name as to whether or not the law-book which had been found really contained Yahweh's will (2 Kings xxii. 14). It is true, also, that traces of this greatest event of the time are remarkably scarce in the book of our prophet. There is only one passage (xi. 1-6) which refers to it. This, however, suffices to prove that Jeremiah, at God's command, placed himself in the beginning at the disposal of the great reform movement. We can hardly find a better explanation of the passage than that advocated most recently by Canon Cheyne,[1] namely, that Jeremiah worked in the towns of Judah, at first, as preacher of the reform. If so, we can easily explain why his own townsmen of Anathoth threaten him with death, if he preaches any longer in the name of Yahweh (xi. 21). For the preaching of the reform demanded the centralisation of all worship at Jerusalem, and this meant the closing of all local sanctuaries, that at Anathoth with the rest. It is not surprising that the inhabitants were extremely incensed at such an injury to the reputation and

[1] *Jeremiah, his Life and Times*, London, 1888.

material interests of their little town. But it was not the danger of death that damped Jeremiah's ardour. He probably soon enough recognised the fact that the cleansing fire of the well-meant reform had not proved to be of lasting effect. For, in that passage, to the command of Yahweh to hear the words of the covenant and to act accordingly, he adds Yahweh's complaint that this command had been in vain, for men had immediately, like their fathers, again broken the covenant (xi. 6 *ff.*). Accordingly, Jeremiah did not share Josiah's enthusiastic faith in Yahweh's help, nor did he approve of his bold resolution to oppose the Egyptians. But he indulgently passes it by, and eulogises Josiah's good and pure purpose, his continual practice of law and justice (xxii. 15 *f.*). He deems him happy, the dead one, in comparison with his son Jehoahaz, who was led away into captivity (xxii. 10 *ff.*),[1] and, at the same time, probably happier than all his descendants, who had to experience a still worse fate than his.

---

[1] In vs. 11 he is called Shallum. This may have been his original name, in place of which, at his accession to the throne, he assumed the name of Jehoahaz, as Mattaniah, when he became king, took the name Zedekiah (2 Kings xxiv. 17). But it is also possible that Jeremiah meant to suggest in the briefest way the short duration of Jehoahaz' reign by applying to him the name of Shallum, King of Israel, who reigned but a single month (2 Kings xv. 10, 13-15). If this is the case, his intention was misunderstood by the author of 1 Chron. iii. 15.

Jeremiah's proper activity does not begin until the reign of Jehoiakim, the unworthy son of Josiah. In the very beginning of this king's reign the prophet opposes the faith in the inviolability of the Temple (ch. vii.; cf. ch. xxvi.). Such trust is vain if men at the same time steal and murder, commit adultery and perjure themselves, sacrifice to the Baal and follow after strange gods (vii. 9). All burnt offerings and sacrifices are vain, for Yahweh had not demanded sacrifice from His people when He led it out of Egypt, but obedience and walking in the way of God (vii. 21–23).

We here stand at a decisive turning-point. In these words of Jeremiah prophetism declares the compact with the priesthood which it had made in Deuteronomy to be null and void. It goes its own way again, alone, the way which Amos had long ago prepared. Salvation is to be expected not from laws and external ordinances, but only from conversion of the heart and will to a true morality. The direct continuation of these assertions lies in the later prophecy (xxxi. 31–34), in which, over against the old covenant, Jeremiah sets a new covenant, which is to be written in the heart and mind of the House of Israel. It is, to be sure, the covenant made at Sinai that is here referred to under the title "old covenant"; but the word, as Jeremiah meant it, holds good of Josiah's covenant also, which, after all, was only a renewal of that made on Sinai.

It is easy to understand that Jeremiah made bitter enemies of the priests by this termination of the contract. But at the same time the fissure which had divided the prophetic party for more than two hundred years opens up again. Not only the priests but "the priests and prophets" wish to put Jeremiah to death for prophesying against the Temple, and only the intervention of some of the nobles saves his life (xxvi. 7 *f.*, 16 *ff.*). Poor Uriah, whom Jehoiakim brought back from Egypt and put to death for the same crime (xxvi. 22 *f.*), is the last prophet that we find at Jeremiah's side. All the others whom we meet in his book (chs. xxviii., xxix. 21 ; *cf.* in general xxiii. 9-40) belong to the popular prophets, who prophesy salvation where there is none and lead the people on to destruction. These prophets had so much the upper hand and were so exclusively listened to that the Book of Lamentations knows only such misleaders of the people (ii. 14, iv. 13 *ff.; cf.* ii. 9). It knows nothing at all of the true prophet Jeremiah.[1] It was only the stubborn unbelief which met him from this time on that made Jeremiah a writing prophet, exactly as similar

---

[1] This is the best proof that the Book of Lamentations was not written by Jeremiah, which, indeed, the original text never claims.

unbelief had so made Amos, a century and a half earlier. For it was not until the fourth year of Jehoiakim that Jeremiah received the command to write down his prophecies " from the beginning to the present day," that is, the content of more than twenty years' work. Then he dictated them to his friend Baruch, who, in turn, read them publicly before a large concourse of people which had assembled at the Temple on the occasion of a fast. On this first audience they created a profound impression; but they did not touch the heart of King Jehoiakim. After the leaves had been read to him, he had them one by one cast into the fire, and sent to arrest the prophet in order that he might be thus rendered harmless (Jer. xxxvi.).

We may pause at this example of extreme obduracy and spare ourselves the details of Jeremiah's labours and sufferings. He was fated to work wholly in vain, to see no fruit of his labours, not even the smallest. He uttered repeated warnings against alliance with Egypt, but in vain. He urged the last weak king, Zedekiah, again and again, to surrender Jerusalem to the Chaldeans, so as at least to save his own life and the lives of his people; but all was in vain. He was repaid for this well-meant advice with maltreatment and slander, with imprisonment and peril of life. But he did not allow himself to be disconcerted by such misfortunes, and events took their inexorable course. This failure to secure belief in his mission was Jeremiah's lot even after the fall of Jerusalem. His companions, against his advice, determined to emigrate to Egypt and dragged him unwillingly along into the foreign land (chs. xlii., xliii.). There they practised idolatry in defiance of him (ch. xliv.); and it may be that the martyr-death which he had so often escaped in Jerusalem overtook him in Egypt.

And yet at his call he was commissioned not only to tear up and to overthrow, but also to build and to plant (i. 10). How far did Jeremiah fulfil this task also? How far did he become one of the firm pillars on which post-exilic Israel, Judaism, could rear itself anew? He became such a pillar, first of all, because *his* prophecies were completely confirmed by the events. If no single prophet had foreseen this catastrophe, but if all had prophesied salvation in Yahweh's name, the Yahweh religion would perhaps have perished without a trace. But Israel now recognised that the enemy had not conquered against Yahweh's will, but had only carried out His purpose. Yahweh was again not the vanquished, but the victor. He had punished His misled and disobedient people, exactly as He had announced beforehand through His prophet Jeremiah. The road to new salvation lay in new obedience.

Of such new salvation Jeremiah had, indeed, sadly little to announce. Salvation, according to him, Josiah had experienced in that he had died before worse times set in (xxii. 10). Salvation he had promised to Zedekiah on condition of his abandoning hope and surrendering to the Chaldeans, but this salvation consisted simply in the fact that he should not lose his life and that Jerusalem should be preserved (xxxviii. 17 *f. al.*). He could offer nothing more. When Baruch, the only man who remained faithful to him, bewails his bitter lot, he is rebuked by Yahweh for demanding more than his life in such grievous times (ch. xlv.). Those who had been carried off captive with Jehoiachin cherish in the far-off land sanguine hopes of the speedy fall of the Chaldean kingdom and of a return home. But Jeremiah writes a letter to them in which he blasts all these hopes, and exhorts the exiles to make themselves comfortable in the foreign land. They must build houses and plant gardens, contract marriages and bring up children, seek the prosperity of the land of their exile and pray for it, for a better fate is not allotted them (xxix. 4 *ff.*).

For this attitude Jeremiah was denounced before the Jerusalem authorities, and to it he is indebted for the reputation of being a bad patriot, a reputation which has clung to him up to this day. It is true that he does not appear to attach the slightest value to those great blessings of a people, freedom and power. Nowhere in his discourses do we find the hope of a splendid future, of a restoration of the kingdom, and other glittering expectations such as we meet with in other prophets. But here again *his* picture of the future proved true, while those brilliant hopes were sadly disappointed. Jeremiah is the true prophet of those *little* things which awaited Israel after the exile, of wretched conditions such as Haggai, Zechariah, and Malachi bear witness to. Perhaps the most affecting scene in the whole tragedy of Jeremiah's life is that which is related in chapter xxxii. (verse 6 *ff.*). Jerusalem is besieged by the Chaldeans for the last time; Jeremiah, deprived of his liberty, lies shut up in the court of the prison; his cousin Hanamel of Anathoth comes to him and requests him to purchase his property in this town, he being the lawful redeemer.[1] Thus the very same people who sought Jeremiah's life still find him good enough to make a profitable bargain with. For if the whole land goes to ruin, a field will be worthless, while men can easily hide ready money and carry it with them wherever they may go. But instead of scornfully refusing Hanamel's request, Jeremiah complies with

---

[1] *Cf.* Ruth iii. 9 *al.*

it, because he recognises that such is Yahweh's will. He buys the field for cash with the observance of all formalities; he buys it at Yahweh's command, as a sign that some time in the future houses and fields and vineyards will be bought again in the land which is now falling into the hands of the Chaldeans. But in the long sermon of consolation in which this symbolical action is interpreted, there is not a word about a restoration of the kingdom of Judah and its royal house, not a word about power and splendour, wonderful fertility, rich offerings from the heathen. Yahweh promises only one thing besides the settlement in the old home again, namely, that Judah shall be anew His people and He Judah's God, that He will make an everlasting covenant with it and will not cease to show it favour (verses 37-40).

A step of immeasurable importance has here been taken, the step prepared by Amos and Hosea. The religion of Israel has been detached from the nation's existence. Israel does not need any more to be an independent people in order to be sure of Yahweh's favour and to enjoy His blessings. The most essential content of the old covenant made at Sinai was the gift of the promised land, the settling of Israel on a free possession. It was only with the complete fulfilment of this promise that Yahweh became the only God of Israel. But the tree of the Yahweh religion had now grown so high and struck root so deep that it no longer needed this outward support. Whether free or subject, Israel belonged to Yahweh and Yahweh to Israel. This was a consolation and a refuge, not only for the time of the restoration of Judah under Persian sovereignty, but even for the period of the Exile.

Further, the way was thereby paved for another and more important step, that from a national to an individual religion, a step which Jeremiah himself took, although unconsciously. Up to that time, the nation, as such, had alone been the beneficiary of the religion. The promises were made only to the people as a whole; the individual was sure of Yahweh's favour only in so far as he formed a part of the people. Jeremiah does not preach anything different. The new salvation which he promises is to fall to the nation as such, whether it forms a state or not, whether it is free or subject. But he himself has experienced another religion and another salvation. Like Hosea, he did not preach by word alone. His whole person, his very body, was a living sermon. The fate which Yahweh decrees for him is complete isolation. They all abandon him, one after another,—his relatives, the king, the priests, the prophets, the mass of the people, and, finally,

even the nobles who at first stood by him. At last
only his faithful secretary, Baruch, remains, and
even he is separated from him by the walls of the
prison. This isolation is Yahweh's will, and is rendered more acute by a number of strict injunctions.
He shall take no wife, he shall not mourn with those
who mourn, nor rejoice with those who rejoice (xvi.
1-8). Thus only Yahweh Himself remains to him
for communion and intercourse. But now we find
what we have never met with in any prophet before
this time. Jeremiah appears in continual dialogue
with Yahweh. He complains, he contradicts Him,
contends with Him, defends himself against Him,
but is ever worsted by Him.¹ Yet in the midst of
his grief and despair he awakes to the consciousness
that the words of Yahweh are really the joy and
rapture of his heart, because Yahweh's name has
been put upon him, that is to say, because he is
Yahweh's possession (xv. 16). " Heal me, Yahweh,
that I may be healed; help me, that I may be
helped, for Thou art my praise " (xvii. 14).

It may be said that the true religion of Yahweh
had no other refuge in Jerusalem, at the time of its
fall, than the person of Jeremiah. Here we find a
man abandoned by the whole world and in the
deepest depths of misfortune, who has intercourse

¹ See vii. 16 *ff*., xi. 14, xiv. 9 *ff*., xv. 1 *ff*., xx. 7 *ff*.

only with his God and finds his sufficiency in Him. We have here the foreshadowing of God's word in the New Testament, " My grace is sufficient for thee, for My power is made perfect in weakness " (2 Cor. xii. 9), and of the grand words of the Psalm: " Whom have I in heaven? And I desire nothing upon earth beside Thee. Though my body and heart perish, God is the rock of my heart and my portion for ever " (Ps. lxxiii. 25 *f.*).

And, as a matter of fact, the future advance of Israel on this general line follows in the footprints of Jeremiah. The piety of the Psalms, of which we have just had an example, connects itself directly with this tendency. Let them speak in the name of the community as often as they will, from their very depths there bubbles up a vigorous spring of individual piety, of a blissful intercourse of the individual soul with God. Many of them were the expression of such a relation before the community ever appropriated them. The Book of Job, again, simply develops further the tragic struggle and controversy of Jeremiah with his God. All the patience, all the godliness, which Israel matured in the midst of the sufferings of actual life, finds its prototype in our prophet. Thus the very same man who stood as " a pillar of iron and a wall of brass " *against* his people during his lifetime (i. 18, xv. 20) became after his death "a pillar of iron and a wall of brass" *for* his people.

But the tender, passive individualism of a Jeremiah could not alone have offered sufficient support for the life which was rising again from the ruins. Even before the fall of Jerusalem, a second personality came into prominence, as different as possible from that of Jeremiah, in fact, directly opposed to it, but on this very account capable of giving Israel precisely that which was lacking in Jeremiah. It was the prophet Ezekiel. We have shown that in Jeremiah prophetism cut loose from sacerdotalism and went its own way again. In Ezekiel, on the other hand, we see the priest who draws up his own independent priestly program for the deliverance and restoration of Israel.

Ezekiel belonged to the priestly aristocracy of the Zadokites. He was a young priest, not of the country, but of the Jerusalem Temple, when, after the first surrender of the city, eleven years before its destruction, he was carried off into captivity in Babylon with King Jehoiachin. He received his call to prophetic office some years later in Babylon, at the very time when Jeremiah's letter combated the deceptive hopes of the exiles (Jer. xxix.).

Up to the destruction of Jerusalem Ezekiel's

preaching had only one object, namely, to prove Judah's guilt and to show the necessity of inexorable punishment. Going far beyond what is found in Deuteronomy, he carries Israel's guilt back to the past, to the very beginnings of the nation. The people have practised idolatry from Egypt on, and things have gone from bad to worse. Samaria has suffered the penalty for her sins. Jerusalem, however, has not taken warning, but has acted more wickedly than her sister (chs. xvi., xxiii.). And their fathers were not the only guilty ones. The present generation is every whit as guilty as they. Heathen abominations are practised at the Temple itself (viii. 14 *ff.*). Therefore men must not imagine that they suffer for the guilt of others. Yahweh punishes every individual with death for his own sin, and bestows on him life for his own righteousness (xviii., xxxiii. 10-20). Thus the consciousness of guilt is heightened to the extreme. The prophet is convinced that he has thereby done his duty,[1] and looks forward to the fulfilment of his people's destiny with a coolness and a calm which contrast vividly with the harrowing spiritual struggles of Jeremiah.

But as soon as the news of the fall of Jerusalem arrives (xxxiii. 21 *f.*) his whole attitude changes. He becomes a prophet of salvation, he thinks only

[1] See iii. 16 *ff.*, xxxiii. 7-9.

of the restoration of the nation which has been cast down and apparently annihilated. This restoration in Ezekiel does not appear in the shadowy background, under a servile form and pitiable conditions, as in Jeremiah. On the contrary, by miraculous deeds, Yahweh will raise up His land and His people in glory and splendour. He will not do this for Israel's sake, because of its merits, nor even from motives of mercy and love, but for His own sake, "that His name may no longer be profaned among the heathen" (xxxvi. 16–23, 32). Thus here too the prophet is bent on humbling his people to the uttermost, and making the gulf which separates it from its God as wide as possible. The God of Ezekiel is not the God of Jeremiah, whose relations to His prophet are those of a fellow-man or a father, and who even holds converse with him. Ezekiel throws himself on his face when he receives his revelations, and the fixed form of address, "Son of man," reminds him again and again of the measureless distance which separates him from Yahweh. We see here the priest who is accustomed to draw near what is holy with awe, and only after having performed minutely the prescribed rites of purification and sanctification.

And the holiness of God as well as that of His worshippers is really conceived of by Ezekiel as something thoroughly objective. This conception goes back beyond Isaiah to the oldest times. Holiness is material purity, unholiness is impurity, contamination, infection. Accordingly the important thing for regenerate Israel was simply to keep itself and all that was holy pure from all fresh infection by the impure, the heathenish. We have seen that this was the chief concern even for Deuteronomy. In the prophecies and visions of Ezekiel regarding the Israel of the future it becomes a system which is worked out to its extreme consequences.

Let us look at the picture which Ezekiel draws of the future. In the first place, Yahweh will rescue His scattered people from the dominion of the heathen, bring it home from all the ends of the earth, and bless His land with a new and wonderful fertility (chs. xxxiv., xxxvi., xxxvii.). Edom, which has laid violent hands on the sacred land, will suffer an especially severe punishment (ch. xxxv.). Then the impious horde of Gog advances with fierce rage against Israel, but will be annihilated in a terrible final judgment, Israel not lifting a hand (chs. xxxviii., xxxix.). Thereafter Israel will live undisturbed in its land, free from contact with foreign nations, free from all danger of infection. It is as if Israel were quite alone, as if Ezekiel thought of the whole world outside of Palestine as completely desolate. The fate of all other peoples concerns him and his God only in so far as it is a question of punishment and judgement. Beyond this, all interest ceases.

Now begins the care for the protection of the holy things. The Temple arises on its old site. It is protected by two courts, of which the inner may be trodden only by the priests, and even they must change their garments on entering and leaving it (xliv. 17-19). The Temple precincts, again, are set in a district in which only the priests dwell. On the north of this district are the abodes of the Levites, on the south lie the city Jerusalem and the fields of its inhabitants. On both sides of this whole area extends the domain of the prince (to whom certain prerogatives *circa sacra* belong), reaching on the west to the Mediterranean and on the east to the Jordan. Next the especially favoured tribes of Judah and Benjamin bound this whole territory on north and south, respectively. Then come the other tribes according to rank. Thus the holy things are surrounded by a sevenfold insulating layer and ensured against all profanation and injury. We stand here before a piece of work so fine and studied that it may be compared with the cable, wherein is concealed the speaking wire that connects the New World with the Old.

But the precautionary measures extend much

farther. The persons who are permitted to draw near the holy things are carefully graded. The more menial services are no longer to be performed by foreigners, as in the old Temple. They are assigned to the former priests of the high places, who, under the distinguishing name of Levites, are thus degraded for having served at unlawful shrines (xliv. 9-14). Only the sons of Zadok, that is, Ezekiel's own family, who since Solomon have held the priestly office at the Temple of Jerusalem, are to officiate in the sanctuary itself (xliv. 15 *ff.*). To the old kings there is no royal successor—an arrangement whose object doubtless was to keep the worship free from such fateful influence. A prince only is appointed, whose duty it is to look after the external needs of the Temple, especially the providing of the victims for sacrifice. He has no real powers. A large domain is given him, "that the princes of Israel may no longer oppress the people of Yahweh" (xlv. 8, xlvi. 18). We cannot help thinking that the "prince," like the *rex sacrificulus*[1] of the Roman Republic, owes his existence to the fear of robbing Yahweh of the honour which was formerly paid Him by the sacrifices of persons of so high a rank as kings.

The priests are to act as judges, and, further, to "teach the people the difference between the

[1] Sacrificial king.

holy and the profane, between the clean and the unclean" (xliv. 23), so that every man may take care to avoid all pollution. Comprehensive ordinances are given respecting ceremonies for the cleansing of the altar and the sanctuary (xliii. 18 *ff.*, xlv. 18 *ff.*). The object of these measures was the speedy removal of every vestige of pollution.

This is the ideal legislation of the future, which we find in the visions of the last nine chapters of Ezekiel. Whatever may be our judgment as to its religious value, its historical significance is certainly very great. Ezekiel's ideal kingdom with all its splendour was, indeed, never realised. The great mass of the Jews remained scattered among the heathen. The little community in the promised land, living as subjects of heathen lords in the midst of the heathen, had to be content with the holy city and scant territory round about. But the tendency toward the complete isolation of Israel from the heathen and the avoidance of every pollution, passed over from Ezekiel's visions into the practical law-books. First came the code included in Leviticus,[1] which has such close affinities with these sections in Ezekiel that it has been given, in modern times, the distinctive name, The Law of Holiness.

[1] Substantially contained in the primary portions of Lev. xi., xvii.-xxvi. *Cf.* Haupt, *The Sacred Books of the Old Testament*, Part III., by Driver and White.

Then the great priestly document (P) arose in the circle of the priests who dwelt in Babylon. In this document law and history, closely interwoven, are traced from the creation of the world up to the entrance into Canaan. Everything therein is conformed to the actual conditions of the post-exilic community. For this reason Ezra succeeded in substituting it for Deuteronomy and making it once for all binding on Israel (Neh. viii.–x.). Its precepts were so holy and inviolable that in much later times the adoption of the Book of Ezekiel into the Canon met with difficulties simply because it contradicted the priestly law in many details.[1] We can hardly help smiling at such unconscious ingratitude. For, in reality, the principles and aims of the priestly law are all and in every respect derived from Ezekiel, who has justly been called in recent times the father of Judaism.

We cannot fail to see that the religion of Israel has here taken a decided step backward. An Amos, an Isaiah, a Jeremiah had recognised that God is spirit, and desires to be worshipped in spirit, not by sacrifice and ceremonial rites, but by purity of conduct and of heart. But in Ezekiel, and in the

[1] *E. g.*, not the sons of Zadok alone are to be priests in this code, but all sons of Aaron. It is clear that the former decision could not have been given by Moses, since Zadok was a contemporary of David and Solomon.

priestly law which followed after him, the all-important consideration is the correctness and purity of the cult, the *opus operatum* of the external fulfilment of the law. The old popular religion here stands out in sharp contrast with the ideal religion of the writing prophets; it has carried off the victory in the struggle. Still we cannot fail to recognise a divine purpose even in this. For it is only to the strict, ritually mechanical seclusion from all that was foreign, which Ezekiel taught and the priestly law adapted to actual life, carrying it out into minute details, that Israel was indebted for its tenacious power of resistance. And only by means of this power did it maintain itself and its religion in the dispersion among the nations, up to and beyond the appearance of Christianity. The same power has maintained it down to this very day.

Even those elements of Ezekiel's visions which the sober law could not turn to account, namely, the enthusiastic descriptions of the splendour of the restored Israel, were in nowise lost. The future, it was believed, had still to bring what the present had not realised. Thus the fantastic creations of eschatological hopes, the extensive literature of Apocalypses, reared themselves on the basis of the prophecies and visions of Ezekiel.[1] If the observance

---

[1] In the Old Testament such writings as Isaiah xxiv.–xxvii., Joel,

of the law was a severe tax on the pious Jew every moment of the day, this burden became a delight when he thought of the glory which awaited his fidelity. The strong faith in such a future gave Judaism renewed courage and renewed patience to bear even the hardest lot.

A third foundation pillar for the new structure was laid before the period of the exile reached its end. A third great prophet arose, like Ezekiel, among the exiles in Babylonia. We do not know his name, for his book is anonymous. Since it has come down to us as a supplement to the Book of Isaiah, we are accustomed to designate the prophet as Deutero-Isaiah, the Second Isaiah. The historical appendix, Isaiah xxxvi.–xxxix., is followed by an entirely new book, embracing chs. xl.–lxvi. I shall not discuss in detail the origin of the various sections of this book. I will only say that it appears to me certain that chs. lvi.–lxvi. do not belong with chs. xl.–lv. Therefore I shall leave the former out of consideration here.[1] On

and Zechariah ix.–xiv. form the transition from prophecy to Apocalypse; while Daniel exhibits the latter in its full development. The extra-canonical remains of this literature are far more extensive.

[1] I remark in passing that I am unable to ascribe these chapters to a single writer (a "Trito-Isaiah"), but see in them a collection of pieces by widely different authors, which have been appended to Deutero-Isaiah, precisely as a series of pieces of very diverse origin have been added to the prophecies of the older Isaiah.

Religion of Israel to the
Exile

BM 165
 B83

Budde, Karl

the other hand, I cannot convince myself that in chapters xl.-lv. we are to recognise the hands of two or more authors. In particular, I think it can be proved that the so-called "Servant of Yahweh songs"[1] in chs. xlii., xlix., l., and liii. belong to the very foundations of Deutero-Isaiah. At any rate, if they are detached the rest is unintelligible. If, therefore, they be assigned to another hand, they are older than Deutero-Isaiah and were made use of by him, as Wellhausen and Smend hold. For our present purpose this would amount to the same thing as if we held that the whole section belonged to the same author, as I am convinced that it does.[2]

What, now, that was new and imperishable did this prophet of the exile bring his people? He writes shortly before the end of the Chaldean sway. The Persian king, Cyrus, in whom he recognises the saviour sent of Yahweh, has already entered on his victorious career. So the prophet has nothing to announce but comfort and salvation. "Comfort ye, comfort ye my people, saith your God. Speak kindly to Jerusalem and tell her that her time of

---

[1] Under this name Bernhard Duhm first detached the passages, Is. xlii. 1-4, xlix. 1-6, l. 4-9, lii. 13-liii. 12., from their context and ascribed them to a particular author.

[2] On this question see now my article, "The So-called 'Ebed-Yahweh Songs,' and the Meaning of the Term 'Servant of Yahweh' in Isaiah, Chapters 40-55," in *The American Journal of Theology*, July, 1899, pp. 499-540.

service is accomplished, that her debt is paid, for she has suffered at Yahweh's hand double for all her sins" (xl. 1). Deutero-Isaiah has only one enemy to combat, the want of perfect faith. The deeply humbled and enslaved people dares no longer to believe in salvation. Yahweh has rejected His people and forgotten it; how could He otherwise have annihilated it so completely? Could He reveal Himself anew so gloriously to the wretched remnant? To overcome this faint-heartedness, to turn the weak faith of the people into a strong, joyous belief in the proffered salvation, was the task which Second Isaiah set himself to perform for his contemporaries. He never tires of preaching, on the one hand, the infinity of Yahweh's grace and mercy, and, on the other, His unconditioned omnipotence. Here lies the first point in which Second Isaiah goes beyond his predecessors and works for the future. For Amos Yahweh is the lord of the world and more powerful than all other gods. Isaiah calls the gods of the heathen "nothings."[1] But a theoretical and absolute monotheism is preached for the first time by Deutero-Isaiah. There is not, and never has been, in the whole world any other god than Yahweh. All gods beside Him are nothing more than the wood, the stone, the metal, from which the hand

[1] Isaiah ii. 8, 18, 20; x. 10, 11; xix. 1, 3; xxxi. 7.

of man has fashioned them. With sovereign sarcasm, he lashes the folly of those who engage in such manufacture, and of those who accept the product as a living god, qualified to act and to help (*cf.* especially xliv. 9–20). He sweeps, as it were, all other gods out of the world, and leaves Yahweh, the God of Israel, alone enthroned therein.

The God of Israel! With such a complete recognition of Yahweh's omnipotence the old tormenting question necessarily came up again with redoubled force. Why did this God of the whole world choose only one single little people for His own? We have heard the answers of the earlier prophets to this question. But no one of these is able to explain why God contented Himself with this single people, He who could have drawn the whole world to Himself, and led it to the knowledge of Himself, if He had so willed. It is easy enough to understand why Israel did not go into this question more deeply in earlier times. On the one hand, the real existence of the other gods was acknowledged, and the rest of the world of nations outside of Israel was divided up among them and left to their rule. On the other hand, the natural egoism and the dread of all that was foreign made men satisfied to leave the other peoples to their fate without further reflection. Deutero-Isaiah tears these barriers down. He does not content himself with the particularism of his predecessors. It is the will of the God of the whole world to reveal Himself to the whole world, and to be worshipped by all nations. He chose Israel, to be sure, from among the nations, but only that it might be His servant, His messenger, and His preacher among the peoples. For the Servant of Yahweh in Deutero-Isaiah is not one who renders Him service, that is, worships Him, but one who is serviceable to Him, as the human servant to his human master, who does his work, receives the orders of his master and carries them out obediently and faithfully.

And this Servant, this chosen one, is not an individual. He is the whole nation of Israel, as Deutero-Isaiah repeatedly says from chapter xli. 8 on, even in many passages which do not belong to the so-called "Servant of Yahweh songs" (xlii. 19 *ff*.; xliii. 10; xliv. 1 *ff*., 21; xlv. 4; xlviii. 20; xlix. 3). And although these lyrical sections speak of the positive tasks of the Servant in a specially exalted style, yet they are by no means the only sections which deal with them. I cannot attempt here to correct all the misunderstandings which a false interpretation of our texts has occasioned. The fact that so many contradictory statements seem to be made in these texts with regard to the Servant

The Collapse of Judah

of Yahweh has misled some scholars even to the point of distinguishing several or a whole succession of Servants. But Israel has been the Servant of Yahweh ever since its election (xli. 8), and the prophet looks back upon all these centuries. Is it any wonder, then, that the Servant of Yahweh does not always bear the same features? Was not Israel often enough deaf and blind (xlii. 18 ff., xliii. 4 ff.), stubborn and disobedient (xlviii. 4), timid and fainthearted?[1] And did it not nevertheless continue to be the Servant of Yahweh, bearing in itself the lofty destiny which it was sometime to realise in spite of everything? And this destiny—be it once more said —was to perform the service of the one true God, to cherish the one true religion and carry it forth unto the nations of the world, until they should all lie converted at Yahweh's feet.[2]

By the perception of this fact Deutero-Isaiah had, at the same time, solved the disquieting question of the theodicy, Why did Yahweh reject and destroy His people? This was the question which had per-

---

[1] Ch. xlix. 4. It is to be noted that this last self-accusation stands in one of the so-called "Servant of Yahweh songs."

[2] See Isaiah xlii. 1–4; xliii. 10, 12, 21; xliv. 5; xlix. 6; li. 4 f., 7, 16; and lastly, and above all, the "song," lii. 13–liii. 12. Especial weight is to be laid on the fact that passages from the rest of Deutero-Isaiah are included in this series, precisely as passages from the Songs are included in the opposite series (see the preceding note).

plexed Israel ever since the destruction of Jerusalem. Ezekiel had been able to drown it in a flood of accusations, but he had not been able to solve it, and no restoration of the people could wholly explain why the punishment had been so severe. Now Deutero-Isaiah declares in his very first verse that the people has suffered double for its sins. If one half of its sufferings is the punishment for its sins, for what reason had it to suffer the other half? Did the prophet purposely reserve the best that he had, namely, the solution of this riddle, for the last? Or did the full perception of it dawn on him only at a later time? The former supposition is the more probable, because everything seems to point to this solution from the very beginning. At last it comes from the mouth of the converted heathen and their kings in the celebrated song, lii. 13–liii. 12, which treats of Yahweh's suffering Servant. The preceding chapter, lii., tells how Yahweh will gloriously lead the redeemed people home again from exile. He will bare His mighty arm before the eyes of all nations, so that all the ends of the earth shall see the salvation of the God of Israel (lii. 10). And when the nations and their kings see how wonderfully Yahweh has glorified Himself in exalting this despised and ill-used people, their eyes will be opened and their mouth will overflow with the confession of that which is thereby revealed to them (lii. 13–15).[1] It is to be noticed that the speakers in liii. 1 claim, as an excuse for their previous blindness, that Yahweh's arm had not been visible to anyone up to this time. But it is now visible, according to lii. 10, to "all the nations, to the ends of the earth." Therefore these same nations, these same ends of the earth, now know that this small people of Israel, which had appeared to them so reprobate and contemptible, has had to suffer, not for its own guilt, but for theirs (liii. 1–5). Their guilt was the idolatry to which they had all abandoned themselves, while Israel served the true God (vs. 6). In order to convert them Israel had to die like a "lamb led to the slaughter," that is, had to disappear, going into exile to live among foreign nations (verses 7–9). It could not otherwise come into sufficiently close contact with the heathen peoples, nor would Yahweh have had the opportunity so gloriously to reveal Himself in its restoration. Now He has waked Israel to life again and thereby proved Himself anew the true God. And the heathen, whom Yahweh's Servant, Israel, has brought to the knowledge of Him, now bow before Him in reverence (verses 10–12), and, in this

[1] It is probably best to read in verse 13 *yisrael* ("Israel") instead of the inexplicable *yaskil* ("will deal wisely"), an emendation involving the change of two letters (*cf.* xli. 8; xliv. 1, 21; xlv. 4; xlviii. 20; xlix. 3).

song of humble praise, give Him and Israel the honour which is their due. It is not the prophet's present which is thus sketched, but the glorious future that Yahweh is preparing for His people. The time will and must come when the heathen people will make this confession. This interpretation (which is an old one, but has, unfortunately, been often forgotten) furnishes the only satisfactory exposition of this splendid passage as a whole.[1]

The universalism of Deutero-Isaiah reaches here its completion. The religion of Yahweh is destined to become the religion of all mankind. The suffering of Israel is here explained and transfigured, and, at the same time, a task is assigned the nation, so grand and so glorious that no trial of patience is too severe to bear for the sake of such a destiny. The prediction of Deutero-Isaiah was not at that time fulfilled, and his extravagant promises retired into the background for a long time under the pressure of the post-exilic conditions of Jewish life. But they were not wholly lost sight of; similar hopes arose after him from time to time. The best-known parallel is the late prophecy which has come down to us in two copies, in Isaiah ii. and Micah iv.,— the mountain of Zion elevated above all mountains,

---

[1] This interpretation was revived and defended by Fr. Giesebrecht in the essay, *Die Idee von Jes.* lii. 12–liii. 13, in his *Beiträge zur Jesaiakritik*, 1890, pp. 146 *ff.*

and all heathen peoples streaming thither to learn the will of Yahweh. The plain but attractive little books of Ruth and Jonah are further witnesses of this universalistic tendency, and the proselytism of the Græco-Roman period is the beginning of its victory. But we Christians see in the Gospel of Jesus Christ the glorious fulfilment of the prophecy of the Servant of Yahweh, in Christ's suffering the repetition and concentration of the saving suffering of the people of Israel, which our prophet was the first to understand. Therefore this passage *had* to become a Messianic prophecy, in the narrowest sense of the term, in the Christian Church, and our understanding of it is perfectly consistent with that of the Church.

We have reached our goal. Can we conceive of any sharper contrasts than we find between the world-wide, glowing universalism of Deutero-Isaiah and the narrow, icy particularism of Ezekiel—between the ritualism of Ezekiel and the complete superiority of Jeremiah and Deutero-Isaiah to all external cult —between the resignation of Jeremiah and the enthusiastic expectations of the other two—between the inner life in God of Jeremiah and the world-wide sublimity of the God of Ezekiel? And yet they all belong to the same people Israel and became the three foundation pillars on which post-exilic Judaism reared itself anew. The phantom of the rigid uniformity of the religion of Israel has dissolved before our eyes. In its beginnings this religion had developed out of the most heterogeneous elements; a mass of different heathen religions had to furnish their contributions to it. And at the close of Israel's independent existence we find three prophetic figures, sprung from the bosom of the same people, who confess the same God and yet seem to proclaim three fundamentally different religions.

It has pleased God to give His human children the noblest and most beautiful flower of His revelation, the Gospel of His Son Jesus Christ, not in organic growth from one root, but as the product of the grafting of the most varied plants, which He has brought together according to the dictates of His inscrutable wisdom, and has combined artistically with regard to their individual properties. It beseems us simply to bow in reverence before His providence, and to hear and obey what once was said to Peter, "What God has cleansed, make thou not common!" (Acts x. 15). The study of all the religions of the world is sanctified by the fact that no one of them has been too humble for God to make use of in teaching His people, and thereby bringing us all to an ever deepening knowledge of Himself.

INDEX.

Aaron, 23 *f.*, 206
Abraham, 62
Acco, 49
Achan, 58
Ahab, 20, 116 *ff.*, 129
Ahaz, 131, 143, 148 *ff.*
Ajalon, 50
Amenophis II., 6
" IV., 5, 9
Amos, 123, 128, 133 *ff.*
Ark of Yahweh, 26 *f.*, 52, 89 *ff.*, 109
Asher, 10, 50
Assyria, 54
Astral worship, 162 *f.*
Athaliah, 116 *f.*
Athens, 60
Baal, Baals, Baalim, 40, 45 *ff.*, 57 *ff.*, 69 *f.*, 77, 97, 106 *f.*, 118, 124, 189
Baal-Melkarth, 117
Barak, 18
Baruch, 191, 193, 197
Beeroth, 51
Benzinger, *Archäologie*, 66, 163
Bethel, 52, 112 *f.*
Bethshan, 49
Beth-shemesh, 50
Brazen serpent, 156
Budde, K., 48, 52, 79, 99, 110, 168, 209
Burials, 65

Canaan, invasion of, 7 ; Tell-el-Amarna letters, 11 ; the gods of, 45 ; conquest of, 48 *ff.*, 54 *f.*
Chemosh, 114

Cheyne, 151, 187
Circumcision, 65
Cyrus, 209

Dan, 49, 53, 112 *f.*
David, 20, 32, 53, 61, 64, 105, 110, 158
Deborah, 18, 20
Decalogue, 39, 172
Deutero-Isaiah, 160, 208 *ff.*
Deuteronomy, 171 *ff.*
Dillmann, 82
Driver, S. R., 13, 82
Duhm, B., 209

Egypt, tradition of, 3 *ff.* ; bondage, 10 ; exodus from, 10 *ff.*
Elijah, 18, 27
El-Shaddai, 15
Ephod, 112
Ephraim, 10, 49
Ezekiel, 160, 199 *ff.*

Feasts, 41 *ff.*, 44 *ff.*
Frey, *Tod, Seelenglaube und Seelenkult*, 65

Giesebrecht, Fr., 216

Habiri, 6 *ff.*
Hackmann, *Zukunftserwartung des Jesaia*, 158
Haupt, 205
Hebrews, meaning of, 8 *f.*
Hezekiah, 152 *ff.*, 175, 177 *ff.*
Hilkiah, 177
Holiness, 145, 201
Hommel, 6
Horeb, 4, 16, 18, 43

219

Index

Hosea, 45 ff., 57, 124, 128, 133 ff.
Huldah, 178, 187

Ibleam, 49
Isaiah, 144 ff.
Israel, conquest of Canaan, 6 ff.; servitude of, 10 ff.; delivered by Yahweh, 12; worship of other gods, 15; oldest documents of, 21; covenant with Yahweh, 24; desire for deliverance from bondage, 25; overcomes all foes, 26 f.; need of mighty God, 28; Moses its lawgiver, 32 f.; adoption of religion, 35 ff.; faithlessness of, 39 f.; experiences of, 47 ff.; occupation of Canaan, 49 ff.; learns agriculture, 55 ff.; serving Baal, 57 ff.; national god, 59 f.; astral worship of, 66 ff.; people of Yahweh, 133; election of, 146; holy city of, 160; belongs to Yahweh, 196
Issachar, 50

Jacob, 4, 61 ff.
Jael, 20
Jastrow, *Hebrew Sabbath*, 67
Jehoiakim, 181 ff., 189 f.
Jehovah, composition of word, 1
Jehu, 20
Jerachmeelites, 50
Jeremiah, 36, 43 ff., 186 ff.
Jeroboam I., 112
Jerusalem, 5 ff., 105, 110 f.; siege by Sennacherib, 152-154; inviolability of, 156 ff.; fall of, 200
Jethro, 19, 22 f., 32 f.
Jezebel, 116 ff.
Jezreel, 49
Job, Book of, 198
Jonadab, 43 f., 46; son of Rechab, 20, 120
Jonah, 217
Jonathan, 58

Jordan, 49
Joseph, 3, 10, 49 f.
Josiah, 188
Judah, 19 f., 50 ff., 140, 160, 170; collapse of, 181 ff.

Kenites, tribe of Midianites, 19; Yahweh-worshippers, 20 ff.; 30, 35, 52, 60
Kenizzites, 50
Kent, C. F., 126
Kiriath-Jearim, 51
Kuenen, A., 33, 163

Laban, 61 ff.
Lamentations, 190
Levite, 80 ff., 203 f.
Louvain, 8

Manasseh, 10, 49
Manasseh, King, 161 ff.
Megiddo, 49
Merneptah I., Pharaoh of the Exodus, 5 ff.
Micah, prophet, 157
Micah, sanctuary of, 80
Micaiah, 117, 129
Michal, 61
Midianite, 19
Milcom, 14
Moab, 48
Moore, *Judges*, 79
Morality, 33; *vs.* law, 34
Moses, 4 f.; exodus under, 6 f.; called to divine mission, 13 f.; Yahweh discloses Himself to Moses, 14 f.; sacrificial meal, 23 ff.; receives revelation, 25 ff.; legislation of, 31 ff.; creates Levites, 82 ff.; grandson of, 86; law book of, 172
Müller, W. Max, 10 ff., 88

Naphtali, 50
Naville, Ed., 4
Nebuchadnezzar, 20
Nejeb, 50
New Moon, 66 ff.

Index

New World, 145
Nowack, W., *Archäologie*, 66

Omri, 116

Passover, 74
Patriarchs, 15 *f.*
Pharaoh, 12, 105
Philistines, 65, 88 *ff.*, 104, 123
Pithom, 4
Priestly document, 206
Prophetism, 19, 125
Prophets, 88, 93 *ff.*, 102, 122, 128 *ff.*
Psalms, 198

Rachel, 61
Ramses, 4
Ramses II., 4 *f.*, 6, 9
Rechabites, 20 *ff.*, 30, 35, 45 *ff.*
Reisner, George A., 8
Ruth, 217

Sabbath, 66 *ff.*
Sacrifice, 23; human, 62; family, 64, 184
Samaria, 50; fall of, 140
Saturn, 67 *f.*
Saul, 20, 53, 61, 94, 105
Schmidt, Nathaniel, 68
Schrader, 5, 114, 126, 155, 161, 184
Schwalli, *Das Leben nach dem Tode*, 64 *f.*
Semitic Studies, 124
Sennacherib, 152, 154
Shaalbim, 50
Sharon, 49
Shechem, 50 *f.*, 62
Shiloh, 52
Simeon, 50, 84 *f.*
Sinai, 4, 16 *f.*, 18, 28, 43, 52, 54, 59 *f.*
Smend, 209
Smith, G., 126
Smith, H. P., *Samuel*, 99
Smith, W. Robertson, 31–36, 57, 75, 146

Solomon, 105, 109, 113 *f.*, 175
Stade, B., 163, 167
Stade, Siegfried, 8
Steinen, *Unter den Naturvölkern*, 63
Steuernagel, 172

Taanach, 49
Tammuz, 162 *f.*, 166, 184
Tell-el-Amarna, find at, 5; contents of tablets, 11, 114
Ten Commandments, 32
Teraphim, 61, 64, 69
Terebinth, 62
Thebes, 7
Tradition, value of, 1 *ff.*
Treaties, 51

Uriah, 190

Wellhausen, 209
Wiedemann, A., 8
Winckler, H., 5, 6, 88, 114, 123

Yahweh, as divine name, 1 *ff.*; power ascribed to, 12 *ff.*; origin of name, 14 *ff.*; burning bush, 17; angel of, 18; His abode, 18 *f.*; to whom belongs? 18 *f.*; Kenites original worshippers of, 21; covenant with, 24; mountain god, 25; war god, 26 *f.*; weapons of, 27 *f.*; relation to God of prophets, 28 *ff.*; meaning of, 29 *f.*; ethical character, 36; His rivals, 39 *ff.*; relation to other gods, 41; feasts, 42 *ff.*; Yahweh and agriculture, 42 *f.*; instructs His people, 46 *ff.*; angel of, 52; abode of, 54, 57; God of federation, 60; sacrifice of first-born, 62; worship, 75 *f.*, 78 *ff.*; becomes Baal, 77; image of, 87; might of, 92 *f.*; unconditional master, 106; image of, 112; vic-

Yahweh—*Continued.*
tory over Baal, 124; wrath with Israel, 125; morality of, 128, 134; holiness of, 145; Jerusalem, city of, 157; astral worship, 165; head of pantheon, 167; Creator, 169; centralisation of worship, 173 *ff.*; belongs to Israel, 196; servant of, 209, 212 *ff.*; omnipotence of, 210
Yahweh religion, origin of, 1 *ff.*, 30; ethical development, 35 *ff.*
Yahwism, 52, 69, 72
Yahwist, 21

Zadok, 176, 204, 206
Zedekiah, 182 *ff.*, 191, 193

BIBLICAL PASSAGES.

I. OLD TESTAMENT.

GENESIS.

i.	168
ix., 20-27	71
xvii.	65
xviii.	71
xix	71
— 18	5
xx., 7	95
xxiv., 7	166
xxviii.	112
— 22	113
xxxi., 19, 30	61
xxxiv.	81, 84
xxxv.	10, 65, 112
— 1-4	62
xl., 15	8
xlix., 5-7	84
l.	65

EXODUS.

i., 11	4
— 19	8
iii.	17
— 4	17
— 13	14
v., 14	39
vi., 2	14
xii., 1-14	74
— 9	75
— 21-28	74
xiii., 3-10	74
xv., 20	95
xviii.	22, 33
xix.	27
xx.	172
xxi.	63, 170

EXODUS (CONTINUED).

xxi., 2	8
— 2-6	63
— 6	64
xxii., 6	34
xxiii.	46, 63, 170, 172
— 20	18
xxiv., 7	63
xxxii., 26-29	81
— 26	82, 87
— 29	82
— 34	18
xxxiii., 1-3	18
xxxiv.	39, 46, 74, 172

LEVITICUS.

xi.	205
xvii.-xxvi.	205
xxiii.	42

NUMBERS.

x., 29	19
— 35	26
xi., 26	95
xxviii.	42
xxxi., 25	32

DEUTERONOMY.

iv., 19	174
vii., 1	173
x., 8	82
xii.	175
xiii., 2-5	130
— 3, 8, 14	173
xv., 17	63

DEUTERONOMY (CONTINUED).

xvi.	42
— 21	176
xvii., 3	174
xviii., 15	95
— 20-22	132
xxxiii., 8-11	81
— 9	83

JOSHUA.

v., 10-12	74
— 63	48
vii.	58
— 16	34
ix.	51
x., 12	165
xiii., 13	48
xv., 13-19	48
xvii., 14-18	48
xix., 42	53
— 47	48
xxiv.	65
— 14	15

JUDGES.

i., 3	85
— 16	19
— 19	49
— 32, 33	51
— 34	53
ii.	53
— 1, 5 *b*	52, 78
— 11	40
iv., 4	95
— 17	20
v., 4	18, 27
— 4-20	165
— 24	20
vi.	103, 107
— 8	95
— 11	28
x., 2, 5	65
xii., 10, 12, 15	65
xiii., 2	28
xvii.	51, 53, 79, 85
xviii.	51, 53, 79, 112
— 30	86

RUTH.

iii., 9	194

1 SAMUEL.

i.; ii	23
—; iii	86
—; iv	34, 52
iii.	95
iv.	90
iv; vi	78
— 7	27
vii.	94
— 1	90
viii.	94
— 8	40
ix.	23
— 9	96
— 11	96
x., 1-16	94
— 5	90, 96
— 17	94
xi.	94, 99
— 6	28
xiii., 4	90
xiv., 3	112
— 18, 24, 33, 36, 38, 41, 45,	99
— 38	34, 58
xv., 6	20
xix., 11-17	61
xx., 5	66
— 6	64
xxii., 26	27
xxiii., 6, 9	112
xxv., 28	27, 104
xxvi., 19	53, 124
xxvii., 10	20
xxx., 22	32
— 29	20
xxxi., 10	105

2 SAMUEL.

— 6	165
v., 24	28, 104
vi.	109
viii., 17	176
xi., 2	27

2 SAMUEL (CONTINUED).

xv., 24	27, 176
xxi	105
xxiv	109
— 16	155

1 KINGS.

ix., 15	105
— 20	106
xi	124
— 1	113
xv., 18	116
xvii., 24	106
xviii., 11	139
— 19	97
— 24	92
— 38	27
xix	18, 43
— 11	27
xxi	119
xxii	129

2 KINGS.

ii., 26	186
iii., 4	120
iv., 23	66
v., 17	115
viii., 7	126
ix., 10	121
— 11	97
x	44
— 15	20
xii., 18	126, 143
xiii., 7	126
xv., 10	138
— 10, 13-15	188
xvi., 7	149
xvii., 6	139
— 25	54
xviii., 2	152
— 4	156
— 13	152
xix., 35	155
xx., 6	152
xxi., 2, 16	162
— 5	163
xxii., 3	177

2 KINGS (CONTINUED).

xxii., 12	178
— 14	187
xxiii., 11	162
— 26	161
— 29	180
xxiv., 3, 20	161
— 13	188
xxxiii., 31-34	181

1 CHRONICLES.

ii., 55	21
iii., 1	110
— 15	188
vi., 11-13, 18-20	86
xi., 4	5

2 CHRONICLES.

xxxiii., 10-19	167

EZRA.

i., 2	166

NEHEMIAH.

i., 4	166
ii., 4, 20	166
viii.; x	206

PSALMS.

xviii	27
lxxiii., 25, 26	198

ISAIAH.

i., 2	146
— 2-20	154
— 11-15	144
ii.	216
— 6	146
— 12	145
— 8, 18, 20	210
iii., 16	145
v., 1-7	146
— 13	148, 150
vi.	146, 153
— 1	147, 159

ISAIAH (CONTINUED).

vi., 5	146
— 1, 5, 6, 8, 11	147
vii.	149
— 3, 13	147
— 9	150
— 11	148
viii.	131
— 1-3, 5, 11, 17	147
— 9	148
— 16, 17	150
— 18	158
ix., 1-6	153
— 6	147
— 7	145
x., 5	124, 165
— 10, 11	210
— 12, 28	155
xii., 2	148
xiv., 1	84
— 24-27, 28-32	155
— 28	148
xviii.	155
— 4	148
— 7	158
xix., 1, 3	210
xxi., 9	158
xxii., 1-14	154
— 14	155
xxiv.; xxvii.	207
xxix., 1-6, 7	155
xxx., 1-5	154
— 7	155
xxxi., 1	154
— 4	155
— 7	210
xxxvi.; xxxix	208
xxxvii., 27-29, 33-35	155
— 36	155
xl.; lv	208, 209
xl., 1	210
xl.; lxvi	208
xli., 8	212, 213, 215
xlii., 1-4	209, 213
— 18	213
— 19	212
xliii., 4	213
— 10	212

ISAIAH (CONTINUED).

xliii., 10, 12, 21	213
xliv., 1	212
— 1, 21	215
— 9, 20	211
xlv., 4	212, 215
— 5	213
xlviii., 4	213
— 20	212, 215
xlix., 1-6	209
— 3	212, 215
— 4	213
— 6	213
l., 4-9	209
li., 4, 5, 7, 16	213
lii., 10	214, 215
— 12, 13	216
— 13-15	215
— 13; liii., 12	209, 213, 214
liii., 1-12	215
lvi., 6	84
—; lxvi.	208

JEREMIAH.

i., 10	192
— 18	198
ii., 5	161
— 23	70
v., 14	45
vii., 2	184
— 4	157
— 9, 13, 21	189
— 16	184, 197
— 18	162
— 21	184
— 29	184
viii., 2	162
— 14	184
ix., 13	70
xi., 1-6, 21	187
— 6	188
— 14	197
xiii., 27	184
xiv., 9	197
xv., 1	197
— 4	161
— 16	197
— 20	198

Biblical Passages

JEREMIAH (CONTINUED).

xvi., 1-8	197
xvii., 14	197
xix., 13	162
xx., 7	197
— 10	195
xxii., 10, 11, 15	188
xxiii., 9-40	190
xxvi	157, 189
— 7, 8, 16-18, 22, 23	190
— 11, 16	157
— 18	103, 157
xxviii	190
— 8-10	132
xxix	199
— 4-6	195
— 21	190
— 26	97
xxxi., 29	161
— 31-34	189
xxxii	194
— 37-40	195
xxxv	20
xxxvi	191
xxxviii., 17, 18	195
xlii	192
xliii	192
xliv	192
— 15	162
xlv	195
li., 59-64	182

LAMENTATIONS.

ii., 4, 9, 14, 13-15	190
v., 7	161

EZEKIEL.

iii., 16	200
vi., 13	184
viii., 14	166, 200
— 14, 16	162
xi	160
xvi	200
xviii	200
— 2	161
xx	40
— 26	62

EZEKIEL (CONTINUED).

xxi., 26	61
xxiii	200
xxxiii., 7-22	200
xxxiv	202
xxxv	202
xxxvi	202
— 16-23, 32	201
xxxvii	202
xxxviii	202
xxxix	202
xliii., 1	160
— 18	205
xliv., 9-17	204
— 17-19	203
— 23	205
xlv., 8	204
— 18	205
xlvi., 18	204

HOSEA.

ii., 13	66
— 15	10
— 15, 19	70
iii., 4	61
v., 10	46
— 16	47
— 25	47
viii., 13	10
ix., 3	10
— 7	97
xi., 1, 5	10
— 2	70
xii., 9, 13	10
xiii., 4	10

AMOS.

i., 3	136
ii., 10	10
iii., 1	10
— 2	134
iv., 6	145
— 13	123
v., 1	135
— 8	123
— 18	145
— 21-24	145

Biblical Passages

AMOS (CONTINUED).
v., 21-25	135
— 26	68
vii., 4	123
— 13	113
viii., 5	66
— 9	165
ix., 2	123, 165
— 6	123
— 7	10, 123, 134
— 11-15	135
x., 25	10

JONAH.
i., 9	166

MICAH.
iii., 12	157
iv	216

HABAKKUK.
i., 2-4, 6-17; ii., 1-4, 5 ff.	179
iii	27

ZEPHANIAH.
i., 5	162
— 8	164

ZECHARIAH.
ix.; xiv	208
x., 2	61

II. NEW TESTAMENT.

ST. LUKE.
x., 33	141
xvii., 16	141

ST. JOHN.
iv., 39	141

ACTS.
viii., 5	141
x., 5	216

2 CORINTHIANS.
xii., 9	198

REVELATION.
xxi	160

Recent Publications.

CHRISTIANITY AND ANTI-CHRISTIANITY IN THEIR FINAL CONFLICT. By SAMUEL J. ANDREWS, author of "The Life of Our Lord upon Earth," etc. 8°. $2 00

"This is in many respects a remarkable book. It deals with the important Bible truths, of which little has been heard of late. The same scholarly breadth and thoroughness which characterize the author's 'Life of Christ' are stamped also on this work. . . . The book deserves a thoughtful reading by all Christians."—*The Observer.*

HEROES OF THE REFORMATION.

A series of biographies of the leaders in the Protestant Reformation, men who, while differing in their gifts, were influenced by the same spirit. The series is edited by SAMUEL MACAULEY JACKSON, D.D., LL.D., Professor of Church History, New York University. Each fully illustrated. 12° $1 50

1.—**MARTIN LUTHER,** The Hero of the Reformation. By HENRY E. JACOBS, D.D., LL.D., Professor of Theology, Evangelical Lutheran Seminary, Philadelphia.

2.—**PHILIP MELANCHTHON,** The Protestant Preceptor of Germany. By JAMES W. RICHARD, Professor of Homiletics, Lutheran Theological Seminary, Gettysburg, Pa.

3.—**DESIDERIUS ERASMUS,** of Rotterdam, the Humanist in the Service of the Reformation. By EPHRAIM EMERTON, Ph.D., Professor of Ecclesiastical History, Harvard University.

4.—**THEODORE BEZA,** the Counsellor of the French Reformation. By HENRY MARTYN BAIRD, Ph.D., Professor of the Greek Language and Literature, New York University; author of "The Huguenots," 6 vols.

For titles of volumes in preparation, write for separate descriptive circular.

THE AMERICAN LECTURES ON THE HISTORY OF RELIGIONS.

Each, 8°, $1 50.

1.—**BUDDHISM: ITS HISTORY AND LITERATURE.** By T. W. RHYS-DAVIDS, LL.D., Ph.D., Chairman of the Pali Text Society; Secretary and Librarian of the Royal Asiatic Society; Professor of Pali and Buddhist Literature at University College, London.

2.—**RELIGIONS OF PRIMITIVE PEOPLES.** By DANIEL G. BRINTON, A.M., M.D., LL.D., D.Sc., Professor of Archæology and Linguistics in the University of Pennsylvania.

3.—**JEWISH RELIGIOUS LIFE AFTER THE EXILE.** By T. K. CHEYNE, of University of Oxford.

4.—**THE RELIGION OF ISRAEL TO THE EXILE.** By KARL BUDDE, of the University of Strasburg, Germany.

G. P. PUTNAM'S SONS, New York and London.

By W. M. RAMSAY.

THE CHURCH IN THE ROMAN EMPIRE BEFORE A.D. 170.

With Maps and Illustrations, 8vo $3.00

"It is a book of very exceptional value, Prof. Ramsay is a real scholar and of the very best type of scholarship. A thoroughly good book ; a product of first-hand and accurate scholarship ; in the highest degree suggestive ; and not only valuable in its results, but an admirable example of the true method of research."
—*The Churchman.*

ST. PAUL THE TRAVELLER AND THE ROMAN CITIZEN.

With Map, 8vo $3.00

"A work which marks an important step in advance in the historical interpretation of St. Paul. . . . It is an immense gain to have the narrative lifted from the mean function of being an artful monument and mirror of a strife internal to Christianity which it seeks by a process, now of creation, now of elimination, to overcome and to conceal, to the high purpose of representing the religion as it began within the Empire and as it actually was to the Empire and the Empire to it. . . . Professor Ramsay has made a solid and valuable contribution to the interpretation of the Apostolic literature and of the Apostolic age—a contribution distinguished no less by ripe scholarship, independent judgment, keen vision, and easy mastery of material, than by freshness of thought, boldness of combination, and striking originality of view."—
The Speaker.

IMPRESSIONS OF TURKEY DURING TWELVE YEARS' WANDERINGS.

8vo $1.75

"No conception of the real status of Turkey is possible unless something is understood of 'the interlacing and alternation of the separate and unblending races.' . . . Such an understanding is admirably presented in Prof. Ramsay's book, which gives a near and trustworthy insight into actual Turkish conditions."
—*N. Y. Times.*

WAS CHRIST BORN AT BETHLEHEM?

A Study in the Credibility of St. Luke. Part I. The Importance of the Problem. Part II. The Solution of the Problem. 8vo, $1.75

"The work is one of which students of biblical criticism will need to take account. It is absolutely candid and straightforward, thorough and discriminating, and courteous to other scholars whose conclusions it sees most reason to condemn. It is a fine piece of work."—*The Congregationalist.*

HISTORICAL COMMENTARY UPON THE EPISTLE TO THE GALATIANS.

8vo $1.75

G. P. PUTNAM'S SONS, NEW YORK AND LONDON.

www.ingramcontent.com/pod-product-compliance
Lightning Source LLC
Chambersburg PA
CBHW020757230426
43666CB00007B/730